Josie's Girl: Never Give Up Your Dream

Josie's Girl: Never Give Up Your Dream

A MEMOIR OF LOVE, LIFE, LOSS, TRIUMPH, AND GOD

First Edition

Dr. Ozell Greer-Cooper

Foreword by Bishop George Dallas McKinney, Ph.D. D.D.

Contributions by Anita J. Cooper-Roberts

Illustrated by Heavynn Gibbs

ISBN-13: 9781987613124
ISBN-10: 1987613120

He that dwelleth in the secret place of the Most High shall
abide under the shadow of the Almighty. I will say of the Lord,
He is my refuge and my fortress: my God; in him will I trust.
Surely, he shall deliver thee from the snare of the fowler, and
from the noisome pestilence. He shall cover thee with his
feathers, and under his wings shalt thou trust: his truth shall
be thy shield and buckler. Thou shalt not be afraid for the
terror by night; nor for the arrow that flieth by day; Nor for the
pestilence that walketh in darkness; nor for the destruction
that wasteth at noonday. A thousand shall fall at thy side, and
ten thousand at thy right hand; but it shall not come nigh thee.
Only with thine eyes shalt thou behold and see the reward
of the wicked. Because thou hast made the Lord, which is
my refuge, even the Most High, thy habitation; there shall
no evil befall thee, neither shall any plague come nigh thy
dwelling. For he shall give his angels charge over thee, to keep
thee in all thy ways. They shall bear thee up in their hands,
lest thou dash thy foot against a stone. Thou shalt tread upon
the lion and adder: the young lion and the dragon shalt thou
trample under feet. Because he hath set his love upon me,
therefore will I deliver him: I will set him on high, because he
hath known my name. He shall call upon me, and I will answer
him: I will be with him in trouble; I will deliver him and honor
him. With long life will I satisfy him and shew him my salvation ".

(Ps. 91)

This journal is dedicated to my children, grandchildren, great-grandchildren, great-great-grandchildren, and the future generations to come. I am grateful to God for the gift of longevity; it is an answer to my lifelong prayer. I am blessed to have witnessed four generations come forth. May this memoir help you to see your own journey with greater clarity. I pray the ninety-first Psalm for you each morning that God will bless and keep you under the shadow of his mighty wings.

Thank You

Thank you to everyone who contributed pictures and information, proof-read and edited, gave suggestions and encouragement on my journey to publish this memoir. Thank you to Bishop George Dallas McKinney and lady B.J, for their contribution, and the editors and creative team at Create Space for helping to bring this story together. Thank you to my granddaughter Heavynn Gibbs for drawing the beautiful picture, and Anita Cooper-Roberts for not giving up on my dream to tell this story.

It's not what you become in life.
It's who you become on the journey.
A.R. Bernard

The image, "Josie's Girl" is a depiction of little Ozell
traveling an unknown road.
A journey which she must trust God, and God alone.

Heavynn Gibbs – Great Granddaughter of Ozell

Contents

Foreword

This memoir was created from a portion of the journals kept by the matriarch of the Cooper family, Ozell Greer-Cooper. It is the story of a motherless child; whose survival is a Testimony of God's grace and protection.

It was my pleasure to have met Missionary Ozell Cooper more than Fifty-five years ago. She and her late husband Dr. A.D. Cooper were pillars in our community. They were a team and were role models for young couples in our faith community for sixty years. They loved and cherished each other. Only death could separate them. While rearing nine children they planted Antioch Church of God In Christ, which was one of the first churches to unite with the 2nd Ecclesiastical Jurisdiction of Southern California, within the greater Churches of God In Christ faith. Missionary Ozell Cooper and her late husband were servant leaders who were faithful and supportive in their local church as well as in the Jurisdiction.

Dr. Ozell Cooper gives all praise and thanks to God for protecting and providing for her. She acknowledges that God has been her refuge and strength. From early childhood she has been conscious of God's presence. She speaks of the pain and fears that almost destroyed her faith and hope. But God proved himself to be a friend of the friendless and a present help for the helpless.

I strongly recommend this book to those who are tempted to give up their dream because of the vicissitude and contrary winds of life. I strongly urge young couples who are tempted to throw in the towel because of the changing values and cultural shifts related to marriage and family to read this book. "I pray that the author's purpose and aim will be fulfilled; "to inspire anyone in similar circumstances to hold on as God reveals his plan for your life."

Missionary Ozell Cooper has a wonderful legacy of trusting God for seventy-two years of marriage – rearing nine children while serving as First Lady at the Antioch Church of God In Christ, and freely sharing her life with twenty-two grandchildren, thirty-eight great grandchildren, and ten great-great grandchildren.

She was inspired as a young child by her acquaintance with Bishop Charles Mason, Founder of the Church of God In Christ; and the discipline and training of the Church. She is a lifelong learner who received an Associate Degree in Child Development from San Diego City College and a Bachelor's Degree in Bible Studies from Trinity Theological Seminary, and an Honorary Doctoral Degree from American Urban University.

Bishop George D. Mc Kinney
Jurisdictional Prelate

Commentary

Outside, the sun is beginning to peek over the horizon, Inside, my mother awakens to begin her inward journey toward the secret place of the Most High. She journals, speaks in heavenly tongues and prays for her family, her church, the community, and even the nation. Over the past seven years, I have had the honor of gathering and synthesizing her private journal entries. In that time, I have been on a literary journey to capture a lifetime of intimate thoughts about love, life, God, children, and marriage and fold them between the corners of this book simply entitled *Josie's Girl.*

This project was monumental. I often wondered why my mom chose me to take on this task. Maybe it was because of my colorful imagination; maybe she knew that God would grant me a rare gift of time, a season when I was available to say yes; or maybe she wanted to challenge me to travel beyond the atmosphere of my mind, into the ionosphere where untapped skills and abilities exist—she always had a way of doing that! Whatever the reason, I did not take this challenge lightly. To witness her life, unfold on the pages right before my eyes was amazing! Her pen-meets-paper style charted a road map for me to deliver her most intimate thoughts to you. This opportunity was very spiritual for me. I was often gently awakened out of my sleep with vivid metaphors and similes that helped me paint the perfect picture on the canvas that Mom was drawing on.

I envisioned developing this work as an interactive project. To mix a blend of stories with some of Mom's favorite scriptures, to put her writings into historical and cultural context, to make it medically relevant, and to provide pictures that would be etched in your minds forever and space for you to write as the stories awaken memories in your own mind, so that you will begin a journal for those who will come behind you.

But when I read Mom all of this, she insisted, "That don't sound like me!" Her desire was to maintain a raw format. She wanted me to simply take the information, type it, and publish it. But I know my mom. She is not a simple person when it comes to learning about something important. I see how she prepares for Sunday messages. It's as if there will be ten thousand people there. She uses the King James and New International Versions of the Bible (KJV and NIV, respectively), Strong's Concordance, history books, and her iPad. She is the cross-reference queen. So how could I not design this book to challenge the reader to peel off the many layers of her life? But I did it. I suppressed my poetic nature to give a considerably raw account of her life, and I am happy that she challenged me to do so. I began to pay close attention to her, and I quickly realized that the vernacular Mom uses is one of the last foreign tongues indigenous to African American culture. So, it was indeed important that I capture the tone as well as the dialect of her speech. I realized, how she said it was just as important as what she said. In my attempt to maintain this tone, you, the reader will run across dialect-specific words such as "neh 'bout" and "sho 'nuff." You will also notice that Dr. Cooper uses "anyway" and "anyhow" interchangeably. This is important because it's highly possible that my granddaughter, Lailah will never hear this style of speech in our family.

Mom's journal entries have sparked a passion inside of me; they have evoked an array of emotions. Some made me laugh, some made me cry, and some even made me want to take little Ozell into my arms and rock her to sleep. At times I cried, because through telepathy, my mother's raw pain penetrated my heart.

So, the memoir that you are about to embark upon was written to inspire you to keep your own legacy alive as you travel on this journey called life. It was also written so that you could celebrate some of the love, joy, passion, support, and fulfillment that Mom has experienced over the years. You have a rare occasion to have difficult questions answered by this great woman of God; her answers will provide solutions for many generations, solutions that only wisdom and experience can provide. This is not a book to merely read and place on the shelf. Read between the lines; learn the lessons that are embedded within the stories. Read it to your children and their children.

Now please allow me to present to you precisely 63,875 words from my mom, Ozell Greer-Cooper, to you. Please enjoy.

Peace and love,
Anita Joyce

Me at seventy two years old celebrating earning
my Bachelor's degree from seminary

Introduction

Let's look at our society in the modern twenty-first century. We are smarter but not wiser. We live longer but not healthier. We have more but enjoy less. We can go to the moon, but we cannot go home to a good family or visit our neighbor's house next door. We have access to more information but know less of Christ. Tragically, we protect whales but kill our children. We improve the quality of our food but produce less healthy strains for our consumption. We have more religion but less love. We blame others for our personal choices, and we look to ourselves rather than God for the solutions.

Take into consideration the United Nations. This governing body was created to maintain peace around the world, yet we are in the constant midst of war. Sadly, most of our wars are strongly influenced by religion and a difference in ideology. In the end, humankind longs for a world full of peace, prosperity, and love.

I am here to let you know that there is a place where we can go to find peace, calmness, prosperity, and love. This search may seem long and hard. But you, my friend, don't have a choice—this search is necessary. Our responsibility to dictate what we desire is crucial to create a better world. I will admit that I desire power. And with this power, I will do something to help myself as well as others. This memoir was written to give you, my family, the power of information to successfully navigate through life with confidence, individuality, and, most importantly, God.

On the other hand, I did not have this privilege because my mother died when I was just six weeks old, so it is obvious I never knew anything about her. This has grieved me most of my life. Therefore, my hope and desire are that no one in my family will ever experience the heartbreak of not knowing me. I want each generation to know me, as a child, as an adult, and as a Christian. I want to let you know some of the things that happened in my life, both good and challenging. I pray that some of these experiences will be a blessing to your lives. I want to encourage young women to commit to raising their children to esteem their father. I pray that even the very young mother can be encouraged to never give up on raising her children in the ways of the Lord. Be mindful when you raise your children; you may be nurturing a senator, doctor, or even the president of the United States. I hope to convey a strong message to young women: "Invest time into your children, and they will be a blessing to you in the end."

Because I married so young, I faced many ups and downs in my marriage, which caused me to miss graduating from high school. I want to encourage you to go back and get a high-school diploma and continue to college and graduate. You can go to school and raise your children at the same time. I love to remind myself that "success means never giving up."

I also want to encourage you to fight for good health, even when sickness comes your way. My formula? I drink plenty of water, eat fresh fruits and vegetables, exercise every day, and think positive to live a full life. I am adamant about this because I have struggled with many illnesses through the years, but over time, and with God's help, I conquered them all. My body was healed from diseases that could have killed me, but God said, "Not now!"

Most of all, I want my family and the world to know how Christ saved me from a miserable life of sin. God had mercy on me, a sinner. He gave me life when he could have ended it. I was consumed with pride and did not want to be saved. Pride had taken over my life, and I was on my way to filling my children's life with that same pride. I thought, "If I raise my children on the upper crust of society, they would be counted."

I wanted to live vicariously through them because I had no one to push me toward greatness. The religion that I was a part of as a child emphasized God, but it did not push children into high society. So, I was going to leave God out of it. But thanks to God's grace and mercy, he filled me with his precious Holy Spirit and gave me a new life in him.

> *"But we all, with unveiled face, beholding as in a mirror the glory of the Lord, are being transformed into the same image from glory to glory, just as from the Lord, the Spirit"* (2 Cor. 3:18).

I want the world to know what a beautiful existence it is in serving God.

Many people have asked me the secret to having a clear mind, a physically fit body, and a strong, sure spirit at my age. It's no secret; I simply practice discipline, a ritual every day that keeps me on the path toward greatness. I don't falter or waver, not even for a day. I meet each morning with prayer and devotion. I fall on my face before God. I journal and listen to positive reinforcement tapes. I tell myself each day that there is greatness in me, but not on my own merit, for it is the love of God that makes me great. I have never wanted my children to have to take care of me, and I stand firm that I will not be a burden to them. I have the God confidence that I will take care of myself until the day the God says, "That's enough!"

Finally, I wrote this memoir because I want you to take a piece of me and carry it with you for the rest of your lives—it is your legacy. This is delicate information that needs to be preserved and passed down to my future generations. The Word of God says,

> *"For He established a testimony in Jacob and appointed a law in Israel, Which He commanded our fathers that they should teach them to their children, That the generation to come might know, even the children yet to be born, that they may arise and tell them to their children, that they should put their confidence in God and not forget the works of God, but keep His commandments"* (Ps. 78:5–7).

I admonish you, do not take your time here on earth lightly; make your own history, and continue the legacy. Now, my children, I invite you to take this precious memoir and allow it to grace your bookshelves for many years to come.

Love,
Ozell Greer-Cooper

CHAPTER 1

Birth to Age Ten

(1925-1935)

The Roaring Twenties was a progressive decade. The little black militant Malcolm X, famous American blues guitarist B. B. King, US Attorney General Robert F. Kennedy, and the witty child Actor Sammy Davis Jr. were all born during that time. The Charleston swept the nation, and President Calvin Coolidge led the United States into a period of rapid economic and social growth. But the most important event at that time was my birth.

My Birth

I was born August 7, 1925, the fifth child to Lonnie and Josie Greer in Emerson, Arkansas, a one-horse town in Magnolia County. But I was delivered by Dr. J. C. Walker from Walkersville, a small subdivision in the rural part of the county. I can imagine that, like any young expecting mother, my mom had dreams for her baby. She nourished me as I grew inside of her for nine months, and I'm sure she told me how much I was loved. With anticipation she awaited the arrival of her precious child. I was told that she labored way over into the night. Papa said that she was at home when I was born. But he never told me that she had any complications with her pregnancy. I believe she did, because babies were usually delivered by midwives in those days. Papa said he knew something was wrong, so he set out walking to Dr. Walker's office to have him come and deliver me. Because my birth certificate says he was my mom's doctor when I was born, it gave me an indication that there were complications with my delivery. Somewhere down the line, I believe my mom consecrated me in the womb because I was told that she was speaking in heavenly tongues as she delivered me. I was told this by a woman who knew my momma. I didn't know her, and I wouldn't know her if I saw her today. She lived in the same subdivision that my sister lived in.

She said, "I knew your mother."

I said, "You did?" because when someone said they knew my mother, I would start asking questions.

She said, "Your mother spoke in unknown tongues as she delivered you!"

And I began to imagine that with the rising August sun, she presented me, her baby girl, to the world. Little did my mom know that six weeks later, she would return to the heavens, leaving me here, on earth alone.

Looking back, I believe that her new role was to gently guide me through life. She had to! It was impossible for me, a six-week-old baby, to understand what truly lay ahead in life. At six weeks old, I could not have known that I would need a mother to fill the loneliness that would consume my days, that I would go through life with a hole blazing through my heart, or that I would always feel like I never "fit in" with other children. How could she have known that I would grow up being teased by the other kids? "Star the cow is your momma!" She didn't know that Star's milk would be my only nourishment for survival and that butter mixed with sugar, tied up in a linen cloth, would be my pacifier. Well, at six weeks old, I was only supposed to worry about falling asleep to the syncopated rhythm of my mother's heartbeat and being hushed by the aromatic scent of her breast milk.

Whereas today my children have immediate access to me whenever they desire answers to life's puzzling questions, I could not have known that I would be on an eternal journey to grasp answers out of thin air. For answers that are simply "a cup of tea" away for most people, I would have to pretend to hear my mother's voice when I asked those hard questions.

After Mom's death, Papa said his life changed. He said that's when his struggles began. It was the end of September the week Josie was buried. Thunderstorms were common at this time of year, but this one was like no other. I was told that rain came down like angry tears from God. I can imagine my strong, handsome Papa wearing a blue serge suit and a Stetson hat, standing straight tall with all the dignity he could muster up. I also imagine him holding a black umbrella and looking down where my momma was buried.

You figure that he had been pierced an injection of reality: a young father, alone, with five small children to raise. He said it was a very trying time for him. He also said I caught pneumonia that same week, but they took me to the funeral anyway. I was so congested that Papa literally sucked the mucus out of my nose with his bare mouth. I have always wondered if the illness that my mother died from had any effect on my health.

Thank God for my grandparents. They gave Papa the help he so desperately needed. Very soon after my mother's funeral, he packed up, took us to Grandma Emma's house, and moved to Shongaloo, a Native American city in Webster Parish, Louisiana, where he began a new life for himself. Papa's life as he knew it was over. All the plans that he and Josie had made to raise their children, live a happy life, and grow old together were cut down like a blade of grass. There was not even a whisper of my mom left here on earth. Everything was buried with her on that hot, rainy September day.

Papa was forced to turn around and pave a new path for himself. In my heart, I believe that from the day my mom was buried until his own death, he was subconsciously on a quest to recapture any measure of the love he had lost. He did not like talking to me about my mother, so I was void of many things I should have been informed about her. I wished Papa realized that my life could have had a different beginning if he had only ended his silence.

GRANDPA STEVE AND GRANDMA BETTY

Papa's parents, Steve and Betty Greer, left Arkansas soon after my mom's death, so I never had the chance to grow up knowing them. They moved to Honey Grove, Texas, and soon after to Sacramento, California, because of some problems that Grandpa Steve had with the Jim Crow people. I later found out that my grandpa was what is labeled today as an activist. He stood his ground with anyone who showed injustices. And let me tell you, there were plenty of injustices shown in those days.[1]

---

1 *Although the US Constitution reads, "All men are created equal," this was anything but true in the Jim Crow South. The phrase "Jim Crow" has often been attributed to caricature of blacks performed by white actors in blackface and was used to ridicule Negroes.*

Those Jim Crow laws made the South a very difficult place for my grandpa to live. You could be hung for just about anything: something as outrageous as throwing stones, skipping a rock across a lake, or making eye contact with a white woman could literally lead to death. At the rate that he was speaking out and rising against white folks, he could have wound up a strange fruit swingin' from one of those strong, beautiful oak trees.

Legend has it that my grandpa Steve was a man of progress with a proud and brave spirit. But I can imagine how fear and uncertainty could have shackled that spirit. But he didn't give up. He refused to be controlled by those unfair laws. He took an epic leap of faith and moved his family 1,742 miles west, to the entry point for most Negroes from the South, Sacramento's west end. Grandpa Steve worked for the largest employer in Sacramento, the railroad. He worked as a train conductor from the time he arrived until he retired. Also, by the 1920s, Negroes were able to homestead, which meant that no one could legally take their property from them or force them to sell it. Grandpa proudly lived at his homestead, 420 T Street, until he died.

> In the 1930s, there were about thirty-three thousand Negroes living in California, 873 of them in Sacramento County; I am proud to say that my grandpa Steve was one of them. I often wondered, "Why California?" But I later learned that California was not haunted by the Jim Crow South. It was a sanctuary state, providing a haven for Negroes fleeing the South in search for a better life. I also learned that by 1925, Negroes and Indians had begun to establish

---

When the laws of racial segregation—directed against Negroes—were enacted at the end of the nineteenth century, they became known as Jim Crow laws. They mandated a type of racial segregation in the United States called a "separate but equal" status for Negroes in education, public transportation, restaurants, drinking fountains, public parks, the US military, and especially the judicial system. This separation practice led to conditions that tried to make Negroes feel inferior to whites. For example, Negroes had to go to the back door of a restaurant, whereas whites went through the front with the same money. White people wanted our green money but rejected our black faces. We were not welcome to dine in. And thereby a culture of hate was created. Extreme violence, intimidation, beatings, and lynching's were unleashed to maintain mental and physical control of Negroes. It was a systematic way to effectively dissolve us from society.

settlements, and under Mexican rule, some Negroes even became naturalized Mexican citizens to attain status in California. Also, men who were skilled as mill workers were recruited from the South with transportation cost provided and housing guaranteed. Black civic leagues and the African Methodist Church were on hand, waiting to help the newcomers get settled.

I want my children to know that they should feel a sense of pride and entitlement in California; that their ancestor paved the way for them to enjoy every aspect it has to offer. Negroes such as my grandpa made significant contributions to California's growth and development. In his own unique way, he carved his footprint into foreign territory for the bet-terment of his family during a time when other Negroes were paralyzed by horror, afraid to take a risk.

My Earliest Memory of Papa, Lonnie Greer Sr.

My earliest memory of Papa was when I was around three years old. I couldn't understand why he had to leave me with my grandparents. I didn't realize that he could not take care of such a small baby and work to provide for all his children. When he did come, he took my sisters and brother but would leave me with my Grandma, which made me feel left out. When I got old enough to take care of myself, he would allow me to go with him sometimes. I looked up to him and wanted him nearby. He never talked about anything much unless he was teaching us to carry ourselves respectable

My handsome papa,
Lonnie Greer, Sr

out of his presence—not getting pregnant before marriage or tarnishing the family name. A good name in those days was traded just like money, so it was a valuable commodity to invest in. A person could buy land on his or her name alone.

Papa also believed that women should be good housewives for their husbands. That they should cook, clean, take care of the children, and obey their husbands. He also held the man in high esteem as the head of the household. The man was to work hard and take care of his family. Papa wanted us to stick together as siblings and respect other people. I suppose he did something right, because to this day, none of his girls have ever been divorced. I'm sure he also never wanted us to experience what he had felt for so many years, a deep sense of loneliness.

Papa Working for WPA

I remember Papa working just for food. It was called the Works Progress Administration (WPA).

> On this day, May 6, 1935, President Franklin D. Roosevelt signed an executive order creating the WPA, just one of many Great Depression relief programs created under the auspices of the Emergency Relief Appropriations Act, which Roosevelt had signed the month before. The WPA, the Public Works Administration (PWA), and other federal assistance programs put unemployed Americans to work in return for temporary financial assistance. Out of the ten million jobless men in the United States in 1935, three million were helped by WPA jobs alone.

Papa would plow the field from sunup to sundown. In my mind, I can imagine it now, that hot sun beaming down on him as he walked acre after backbreaking acre bent over with a long, white sack strapped to his back, picking cotton until his fingertips were bloody and sore. With his personality, he was aimed to finish every bit of those crops. All so that he could provide food and a place for us to stay.

I didn't understand then the sacrifices he made, but I do believe that he fulfilled his promises as a father the best he could. Although he did not fulfill all my desires, he did enough to let me know how much he loved me. I'm sure if he could have done more for me, he would have. When I think about it now, even if we were to have spent every minute together, I still believe that I would have been unhappy, because the void was not from him, it was from my mother. His absence only added to the void that was already inside me.

I now understand that even though he was not there with me all the time, he loved me and wanted the best for me. I know if there was someone at his house who could have taken care of me while he worked, he would come to get me to live with him for good. So, I was happy for the in-between times when he did come to get me.

Papa Being Picked Up by the Law

When Papa would leave the house, he would warn us, "If I don't come home in a couple of days, go to your grandparents' house." One night, I remember being at Papa's house and seeing him leave home and not return. I later learned that he had been picked up by the law! I never knew the details surrounding his arrest because he was quiet about his private life, but because I knew my papa, I could almost put the pieces together in my mind.

"The Jim Crow South had already driven Grandpa Steve out West and had tried to strip nearly every Negro man I knew of his self-worth. A proud look alone could yield the death penalty. In those days the KKK was the judge and jury, and court was held in the woods. So, a proud, confident man like Papa could easily draw negative attention to himself if he wasn't careful.

Unfortunately, because confidence oozed out of Papa like thick molasses, he was a target for those dreadful encounters. If you don't remember anything else that I write about Lonnie Greer Sr., remember this: He was a very proud man! His confidence stretched beyond pride and spilled over into the "I ain't got nothing to lose" category. Because, you see, my papa had endured one of the greatest disappointments that a child in those days could experience with his or her parents. His decision to quit college and marry my mother cost him his relationship with them forever. Not because she was a bad person, but because it just altered the plans that Grandpa Steve and Grandma Betty had for him.

As devoted Baptists, they were committed to the long, rich tradition of attaining high education and social status in the community. The plan for Baptist children was to take the eldest child (Papa) and educate, shape, and groom them into socialites. They would then be released into the world with poise and self-assurance. The expected result was for that child to return home and change the socio-economic condition of the family. This cycle was to continue until that family completely dug their way out of poverty and all the baggage that came with it. Papa was well on that road when he met, married, and started a family with my mom, Josie, a little girl from the country, with a praying momma and a song in her heart: "I know the Lord will make a way somehow." Her family followed the Holiness tradition, focused on those things that were of God.

Although Papa quit college, he still used his limited formal education and intelligence to teach part time. But he had to farm and work the land to support his four children, so his dream of becoming a full professor was never realized. I guess that could be the reason I love education so much; maybe I'm subconsciously living out Papa's dream."

Because Papa was polished and educated, he didn't go around shuffling his feet singing, "Yeasua. Nawsua." He looked everyone straight in the eyes when he spoke to them. When he would go to bale squares of cotton, he knew to the very penny how much he would clear. This level of intelligence was dangerous for a Negro man in those days. I also knew that Papa drank alcohol at times to lubricate his emotions. Although I never saw him drink, I could tell when he had been drinking. He would walk straight with his head leaning to the side. I can imagine it washed away all his inhibitions to express himself to the law, or anyone else, for that matter."

So, when he didn't show up after a couple of days, my oldest sister MaeLee had my other sister Alee pack a sack of my siblings, Alvernia (Al), Frank and my personal belongings, and we headed out toward Momma's house. Alee put me on her back, and we started out on the old Shongaloo Road, walking nearly ten miles to Emerson. MaeLee and Alee would take turns, shifting me from one back to another. We walked through turnip patches and across cotton fields and plodded through the woods. Soon, off into the distance down the long, dusty road, we could see warm, easy going people sitting on the front galley laughing and talking about the goodness of the Lord. We knew that a hug, a hot meal, and a soft pallet made with warm and soft quilts, were waiting for us.

When Papa got out, he came and picked up the older children, but again he left me, because there was no one to care for me while he worked. That's why I grew so close to my grandmother. I followed her wherever she went: visiting the sick, fishing, or going to church. It was all fine with me, just since she had me with her.

I always wanted to cuddle and be spoken to in a soft tone. I longed for a mother to give me a great big hug and kiss me goodnight. Grandmother loved me with all her heart, but she never really hugged and kissed me much. I always seemed to be somewhat at a loss, because although I never met my mom, I missed her so much. I couldn't understand why all my cousins and friends had one and I didn't. I just felt so lonely. Consequently, things that should have been fun to me were never fun, and things that other kids found funny, I never did. I was so serious about my life as a child. My grandmother understood this, so she gave me extra attention. She called me the baby; I was her baby. She balanced my life as best she could, so I'm sure Papa was grateful for that. He never seemed to mind. The two of them got along well. Papa respected Grandma, and Grandma respected Papa. So, I never felt torn between the two.

Farm Living

After my mother died, I was left to be raised on my grandparents' farm. Growing up on a farm was fun. We had to work hard, but it was yet fun. We made our cooking oil from lard that was cooked out of fat pork in a big wash pot. They would first hang up the pig and cut off the best parts to be smoked and cured in a smokehouse. Then they would take the fragments of the pig and peel all the fat off those parts and cook the fat out in a wash pot, and that fat would become lard. With that lard they would cook the skin and make cracklings. And, by adding lye and water to the lard they would make the soap that my sisters washed clothes with. You never seen clothes so bright and clean. We used the lard all winter long.

It seemed that the farm supplied all the essentials for us at that time: fresh vegetables, eggs, milk, hogs, and chickens. We raised our own corn and took it to the mill to be ground into cornmeal. Country life was wonderful. Delicious snacks were at our fingertips: blackberries, huckle-berries, dewberries, and mulberries. We cracked hickory nuts, walnuts, and pecans. All of this grew in the wild. The spring was shaded by sweet gum trees, pine, oak, peach, persimmon, and willow trees. Those trees were so tall and full that even when you walked through the woods at day, it appeared dark.

Deep in the thicket was a good place to hunt for free meat: squirrels, birds, possums, rabbits, and deer all lived in the wild. In the winter, we watched the bayou freeze over, and the woods would neh 'bout filled up with snow. It was freezing cold in Arkansas during the winter, so there was not much to do outside. We would gather around the fireplace and parch peanuts or put our sweet potatoes deep into the ashes of the fireplace to roast them. After our bellies were full, we would fall into a deep sleep to the tap, tap, tap of the rain on the tin roof.

My mom's mother was Grandma Emma, whom I called Momma. Grandpa Frank, whom I called Grandpa, was the husband she married after my grandpa Joe Glover died. They were my protection. Although Momma was my refuge and I fell in love with the reality of living with her, I was crazy about my papa, Lonnie Greer. He couldn't imagine how badly I wanted to live with him. He would come often to see us, but I was still so unhappy. In fact, I was unhappy most of my childhood. Although I had sisters and a brother, I simply felt alone.

Grandma Emma.

My grandmother Emma Ferguson was born just after the end of slavery. Abraham Lincoln was the president at the time, and the Thirteenth Amendment of the US Constitution had just declared that slavery was formally abolished. Grandma Emma had a sister named Charles Ann and two brothers, Scott and Sonny Boy. She originally married Joe Glover and reared three children: Sue Willie, Essie, and Josie. After grandpa Joe passed away, she married Frank Washington and had seven more with him: Burt, Addie, Archie Dean, Lizzie Mae, Rosie Lee, Luther, and Emma Lee.

Although we have yet to discover the particulars of exactly how our ancestors arrived in the state of Arkansas, the first African slaves arrived there with German settlers from Old Biloxi, Mississippi. They had originally come from Guinea during the 1720s. However, the number was evidently small because by 1769, there were only 16 Negroes in Arkansas, and in 1818 only 287 slaves and 5 free Negroes were listed as residents in the state. It is conceivable that Momma was a descendant from either the 287 slaves or the five free Negroes.

You had to have met Momma to know just how kind and gentle she was. She was a good example of a Christian woman. She would spread the gospel of Jesus Christ everywhere she went. Negroes knew her as Mother Washington, and white folks knew her as Aunt Emma, but I knew her as a saint. She was the living epitome of "Love thy neighbor as thyself." One of her favorite scriptures was Romans 1:16 (KJV):

"For I am not ashamed of the gospel of Christ: for it is the power of God unto salvation to everyone that believeth; to the Jew first, and also to the Greek."

Momma was a great cook. She would can peaches and make homemade preserves. And when her neighbors would take sick, she carried warm biscuits and preserves to them, even if we had to go through the back door to deliver it to white folks. She would gladly do it, for it was her mission in life. When Grandpa Frank killed hogs or calves, she would divide a portion of the meat and take it to her neighbors. She even fed hobos when they came by. They knew where to go! They weren't homeless; they would just go from one place to the next. When they came to our house, Grandpa might not let them sleep there, but Momma got in that kitchen and cooked for them people just like she would if a preacher was coming for Sunday dinner. My grandmother was something else, and that's why

God blessed her so. She was a great counselor for young women, and she worked as a
midwife. I remember her leaving for weeks at
a time, off delivering babies.

Her voice was soft, and her spirit as sweet
as warm syrup. I can never remember her cat-
echizing me too much. She would go along
with me for a good while before she did, so
I loved her for that. But one day I disobeyed
her, and she promised to whip my behind. So,
I decided to run away, knowing that when I
returned, I was in for it! The mere thought of
that whipping nauseated me. So, I packed my
sack with a handful of clothes and a snack and
headed down into the thicket—not too far.

Grandma Emma,
She was my life

There were woods all around us, and I was always afraid of the woods.
Might as well be honest! I still am.

Because I was afraid, I waited there until it was neh 'bout dark for her
to call my name. Finally, she hollered, "Ooozellll, Ooozellll, come yea,
young'un!" That's when I put on my dramatic performance. I cried and
carried on until she got out the notion of whipping me. I went on home,
ate, and fell asleep. When I awoke the following morning, we went to get
the items I left in the woods the night before. When we got there, we saw
that the wild animals chewed them all up. That made me sad.

All in all, I felt very secure and comfortable with my grandmother. She
was all the mother I knew, and I don't think I could have loved a mother
more than I loved her. She was my all. We were so spiritually connected
that she had a keen sense when something happened to me. She knew
even before I did.

I remember a time when I was at my auntie's house to take care of
her disabled child while they worked the fields. That child was not easy to
care for; he nearly cut my toe off. Momma wrapped it up, but to this day
it is yet deformed. This time my nose started to bleed a river. It flowed all
night long. I hung my head off the side of the bed to keep from messing

up the sheets. The next day, I got up and headed back toward Momma's house because I was worried. Thinking back, I was only seven years old and my cousin didn't think enough of me to send an older person along in case something happened. Children got no respect. They didn't figure kids had feelings. Just after passing the bayou, I saw Momma coming to see about me. There were no phones in those days; people used the grapevine or their spiritual sense to receive messages. I shall always remember the great compassion she had for me. She said she had seen in a vision that something had gone wrong with me. She carried me home and prepared a cold polace cloth to put across my nose to stop the bleeding. A polace cloth was made from linen. It was the same cloth that our flour was packed in. The cloth was dipped in cold water drawn from the bottom of the well. That was the coldest water you could get because there was no ice in our house in those days. Ice only passed once a month during the summer. You could pay twenty-five cents and get some, but there was nowhere to keep it. Momma used the next best thing, well water. She would fill the water to the top of the pan, and then she would continue to dip the cloth in the cold water, wring it out, and place it back on my nose.

Today, I have that same sense about my children. I just about know when something is going wrong; I don't always tell them, I just pray.

GRANDPA FRANK

My grandfather, Frank Washington, was one of the smartest men I knew in his days. He was not a church-going man neither was he spiritual, so he never showed up at church unless he had business with some-one there. In those days, children seldom mixed with adults, so like with Papa, I didn't know anything about Grandpa Frank's private life, but I do know that most people didn't want to see Frank Washington at church or anywhere else if they had business with him. He had dark-liquid eyes and an unreadable face. He always seemed to be on a mission, but I thought he was a great man to commit himself to helping raise five more children ages six weeks to eight years old after he was done raising his own.

He truly was a businessman. Twice he bought forty acres of land and built a house on each parcel. The first forty acres of land he bought was in the lower bottom, and the second one was called the upper place. They both had rich soil because they were near the slews (places where water could stand). There was running water, branches, and many, many oak and pine trees. I never remember using any fertilizer on the lower place where my uncle Archie lived. Grandpa would do what he called "break up a new ground" when he wanted to plant a turnip patch. He and Frank would first saw the trees down, and then they would get the stumps out. He would literally plow that hard ground and get out all the rocks, and the ground was rich enough to plant seeds just as it was. Grandpa would take his hands and sow them turnip seeds, and then he would take a rake and cover them over and just let them lie there. He didn't have to worry about a sophisticated irrigation system or anything.

It was near a spring, and I suppose it was water coming through there somehow, because the spring was up in the hills, and you could see the water coming down through our land. Maybe it would rain, and maybe it wouldn't, but in time we would have one of the most beautiful turnip patches that supplied the entire community for the winter months. People would come from far and near to get turnips out of that patch. He never charged a dime. My grandparents never charged for anything. Folks would just come and say, "Uncle Frank, we would love some turnips out of your patch." And he would give them as much as they wanted.

In the slews the water stood still, but it rained so much in the South that it couldn't get stale. It was called the bayous or swampland. Nothing could get out once it rained in the bayous. That's where mosquitos and other insects would harvest. Not only that—there were big fish also because when there was an overflow, they would swim in, but they couldn't get out, so they would just grow. Don't tell me we didn't eat them freshwater fish! That was some good eating. We had catfish and jackfish the size of my forearm.

Living in the lower bottom, we had a community. There was my uncle Archie, the Cuningmons—they were white people—and the Hudsons, also white. Mr. Hudson's house is where I remember going with my grandmother to take him food through the back door when he took sick. It's like turning on a movie; I can see it clearly in my mind today as if it just happened. Momma would cook baby greens with lots of pot liquor (that just meant it had lots of juice) and put them in a little white bowl. Then she would take freshly baked cornbread and wrap it in a clean linen cloth, and we would walk to the back of Mr. Hudson's house. The back porch was screened in, and he was laying out there, sick enough to die. I remember them saying he had a hole in his stomach. I now understand it was cancer. But when Momma walked through the door, his face lit up; he was happy to see her. Yes, we had a wonderful community in the lower bottoms. But when Grandpa bought his second forty acres in the upper place, we left our tight-knit community and moved to the new house he built. There was not much of a community there. The farms were further apart.

The house in the upper place was not too spacious. But then again, I don't suppose they expected that five more children would have to live there either. It was a five-room house, and there was a dirt road leading up to the galley that had four wooden posts on it. There was room enough under our house for chickens to run around. It sat on blocks, and we had to sweep under the house and keep it just as clean as inside. Outside, we would play "honey and the bee ball, I can't see y'all" while my grandmother and our teacher sat and talked about how to straighten us out. It was not uncommon for our teachers to spend the entire night with us. When they did, Grandpa Frank would kill a turkey, ginney, or a chicken, depending on how long they were going to spend. Grandpa loved to hunt, so there was always plenty of food to eat.

Inside there was a kitchen with a potbelly stove in it. There was also a long handmade table with two wooden benches on both sides. That's where we ate three meals a day: breakfast, dinner, and supper. Now breakfast was the beginning of the day. We ate homemade biscuits, cane syrup, fatback salt meat, and eggs. Dinner was plenty of turnip greens or black-eyed peas with homemade cornbread, ham hocks, and sometimes fried chicken or cured ham, and fruitcake for dessert. Supper was the lightest meal since it was the end of the day; most of the time we had leftovers from dinner. If not, we would have fresh homemade soup, cornbread, and buttermilk. There was never a time I remember not having food.

In the front room, there was a bed and two rocking chairs, one for Grandpa and one for Momma. I remember her burning a gas lantern to read the Bible. The floors were made with green wood from freshly cut trees, so as they dried, the wood would shrink, and we could see the chickens under the house through the cracks.

Grandpa was a very ambitious man. He owned a sugarcane mill where he made syrup for the entire surrounding area. It was always fun to go down the pine-shaded road to the syrup mill. The process was so interesting to me. He had a place where the cane was fed into the mill. The horse then pulled the thing that carried the mill around, and the juice was directed through a pipe into a large pan with a fire under the pan. The fire cooked the juice into syrup. Then the syrup would sit in the pan overnight to cool, and he would put it into buckets to be traded, or Momma would save it for the winter. When people would bring their sugarcane or sorghum to his mill to be ground or made into syrup, he would get so much, and they would get so much. It wasn't for sale. They would just pay him in syrup.

Grandpa built houses and barns, and he also raised and broke horses. He would beat those wild horses till they laid down. I thought it was mean, but I later realized that was the only way they could be broken. He made medicine for sick men by going into the woods and digging up certain roots to boil and mix. He would put the medicine in canning jars and give to men to take it home for themselves. It was a known fact that these men had gone out and gotten themselves into trouble, and Grandpa would fix them before they could face their wives.

He raised cows, chickens, geese, guineas, and goats. He raised prize-winning melons that he was proud of. This is kind of funny. We were all afraid to go in the watermelon patch without Grandpa's permission. He would tell us to stay out from 'round there. But when we wanted a watermelon out of the patch, my sisters, Alee and MaeLee, were smart enough to put on my grandfather's shoes and go in the watermelon patch and get a watermelon. See how smart kids were? They would put on his shoes! I can see Grandpa scratching his head and saying, "How in the world? I don't remember taking a watermelon out of the patch!"

He raised corn, sugarcane, peanuts, greens, peas, squash, and other vegetables. His ingenuity was a great accomplishment for a Negro man in those days. Especially considering it was at the beginning of the Great Depression. With the stock-market crash of 1929, America's song went from "Happy Days Are Here Again" to the "Depression Blues." I'm certain it was challenging at times for him, but his sacrifices made our lives much richer.

CRIPPLING FORM OF ARTHRITIS

At the age of four, I was stricken with a crippling form of arthritis. It was so bad that my papa had to carry me to the doctor on his shoulder. In fact, he said that I did not walk for nearly a year. This meant that everywhere I went, somebody had to carry me. And the doctor did not give me much hope of ever walking again. He said that if I did begin to walk, I would later be confined to a wheelchair before age seventy. What's so strange is that I did not remember being crippled until I saw a man who was carrying his little girl on his shoulders one day. I was grown with kids but suddenly, my mind's eye took me back to the sight of me when I was a little girl and couldn't walk. I thought, "Hum, I remember Papa carrying me on his shoulder like that. I remember how I used to hold his head while he walked me through the woods to the doctor's office."

Praying to See My Mother

When I was a child, not a single day went by that I did not think about my mom. I wanted so badly to know her because all the other kids had a mother to love them, and I never understood why I didn't have mine. I wanted her to be around when I came home from school every day to help me with my lesson. I hated that I never knew her favorite color, how good of a cook she was, what she enjoyed doing as a hobby, or whether she enjoyed gardening. I often wondered what she was doing and how she looked. When I was ill, I would think about her more than ever. Sometimes my childhood imagination would lead me into a fantasy world. I could imagine her cooking me chicken soup and breaking my fever with eucalyptus leaves.[2]

I prayed so hard to see my mother. Not only would I pray, I would dream about her often. My strong desire to dig up anything about her always turned up empty. I had absolutely nothing, not a glimpse. And what was worst, no one I knew could tell me anything about her. I was reminded every time I would see other children with their mothers that I didn't have mine. This made me feel so alone and unloved. I would ask my older siblings, but they were too young to remember her. MaeLee was eight years old when Mom died, so she would tell me how she looked to the best of her knowledge, but she did not remember much. Alee was six years old; she tried to give me some information, but it was not enough for me to hold on to. Alvernia was four, and Frank was two, so they couldn't remember anything.

I often wondered, "Why didn't someone take a picture of my mom?" It seemed like there were faded black-and-white photos of my family everywhere. Snapshots of Grandma Emma holding the King James Bible, photos of my strong, handsome dad, but all images of my mother always

---

2 In its native Australia, the eucalyptus tree is the main food for koalas. It has been used in the past as an antiseptic to kill germs. The oil was used in traditional Aboriginal (African descendants) medicines to heal wounds and fungal infections. Teas made of eucalyptus leaves were also used to reduce fevers. Eucalyptus was soon used in other traditional medicine systems, including Chinese, Indian (Ayurvedic), Greek, European, and in the Southern United States.

fade to black. It was as if the jigsaw memories of my relatives were clean slates when it came to her. Maybe her death was so painful that they simply erased it out of their minds. I don't know.

Sometimes I would go into a daydream so deep that before I knew it, hours had passed. During one of those times, I believed I saw my mom. The dream was lucid; it was raining hard, and I was looking out the window. In the haze of the rain, I saw the silhouette of a lady standing near an old car. She had the same features I had seen in a thousand dreams before. She was walking slowly, and soon she disappeared into the woods. I thought of how hard it was raining and how she never did get in a hurry.

One night when I was about six years old, I asked God to put together the scattered pieces of my dreams to show me the mother whom I so desperately wanted to see. God answered my prayers, and the very image of her came to me as I slept. She was about five feet tall and weighed about 125 pounds. She had black hair and brown skin, and she had a very pleasant look on her face.

For years, I thought I was angry at my mom for leaving me, but I later realized that it wasn't anger; I was just disappointed with life at times, and I missed her so much. If she only knew how I would cry myself to sleep because I could never touch her skin, lie on her breast, hear her soft tone, or have her pull me into her arms and give me the kind of bear hug only mommies can give. No picture to look at or share my dreams and aspirations with. I do thank God that he saw fit to give me something to hold on to as a child. I learned early on not to let go of the vision of her that was in my heart.

I used to think my dad didn't like me. I blamed myself because I figured it was me who took his wife away; I was the reason she was dead. I also thought I reminded him so much of her. That's what I thought. Ain't that something? But I did. Papa never mentioned anything along those lines, but because I thought I didn't look like the other kids, I fixed it all up in my child's mind. I drew this conclusion on my own. Now where did I get that from? Truth be told, I look a lot like Alee. I now know that I had many fantasies in my mind, and nobody straightened me out, so I just grew up with them. That's the way it happened. And why did I spend all that unnecessary time drawing all those conclusions? I don't know. I guess I was simply attempting to satisfy a curiosity.

Birthday Dress

I remember a time when I had just celebrated my fourth birthday. My stepmother, Viola, bought me a brand-new 100 percent cotton dress. I don't remember if it was pink, blue, or what, but all I know that it was bought especially for me and it was the perfect dress for a four-year-old. I waited with fidgeting hands and swinging feet on the galley because Grandma Morgan, the white lady whose farm our family lived on, sent for Frank and Al to come to the big house and pick up the bucket of tea cakes that she made for my birthday. I can hear her now, that slow, thick, southern drawl, "Frrrank, AAAl, y'all come fetch these tea cakes I made for OOOzell."

I had just worn my beautiful dress once, and before I knew it, my beautiful dress was outside on top of the colored clothes pile near the wash pot Alee and MaeLee boiled the clothes in. In those days' clothes were washed outside in a big cast iron pot. A fire was built under the pot, and lye soap was used to clean them.

I watched them wash and scrub clothes, anxiously waiting for the next time I could wear my pretty dress. That's all I could think of. Just then, a wind came up and blew my new dress under the wash pot. I hollered and cried, "Oh my goodness! My dress was gone!" I watched my dress melt into ashes. There was nothing I could do. I sure wasn't going in the fire and get it out. That was a great big thing to a kid. It may as well had been the end of the world. It started off as a perfect day. Grandma Morgan cooked me tea cakes, and I got a new dress. Wow! How could life have been better, before this horrible thing happened? I cried myself to sleep, woke up, and cried some more.

CHILDHOOD EDUCATION

I have always been excited about learning. I can remember as a very young girl, about five years old, I used to try to read the billboards on the side of the road. Clabber Girl baking powder stood out in my mind. This billboard amused and intrigued me. The first word I learned to spell was printed on the front of the same flour sack that my first baby doll was cut from. The sack was large and white with red and black writing on it. This one word stood out to me. I turned that word over and over in my mind. I sat to the kitchen table holding my chin in the palms of my hands. I watched the sack sitting in the corner as Grandma kneaded that dough into a smooth ball and then rolled it flat and cut perfectly round biscuits that melted in your mouth. In the corner of my eye, I could see the word printed on that flour sack; I could not get it out of my mind. At night I would go to bed and even dream about spelling it. To this day, I don't know what the mystery was—maybe because it was such a big word for a little girl like me. I was not satisfied. I turned that word over and over in my mind day and night until I finally learned how to spell "phosphate"! P-h-o-s-p-h-a-t-e. This was not only a great relief but a huge accomplishment to me. I was very proud. Since then, reading has always been my hobby. I love to read more than anything in the world. When I learned to read, the descriptive power of words opened the doors of my mind. I realized that I could shift my mood, travel, and even create the perfect family, all just by reading. I found comfort between the pages of my books. It was my escape. I have always loved reading and education because it was fun; it came naturally to me, plus I had great support from Momma.

At six years old, when I was finally able to go to school, I was excited. But, some of my school days were very difficult for me as the younger child in the family, because I walked four miles to school with my siblings. The walk could be rugged for a little girl trying to keep up. We would have to walk past a slaughter pin where they prepared cows to be shipped to a nearby town. The long stalls were filled with cows ready to be slaughtered. That place stunk! You could smell it for miles. I shall never forget the terrible smell that came from that place.

When Frank and I took old Henry for hunting, I loved to sit on the edge of the pond and paddle my feet in the water, but I was afraid of water. The South is known for its violent thunderstorms; when they would come, it would frighten me because the water would come rushing down the creek so fast that it would branch off and form a new current. The water that got trapped in the bayou, had no way to run out, so it would just continue to rise. The ground would get so soft that hundred-year-old trees would come up from the root and simply fall and land on the bank on the other side of the creek. This created a foot log that could act like a bridge. Sometimes it would rain so long that the water would rise almost up to that log. Our walk to school required that we crossed it, and it was wet and muddy, and that frightened me. I was only a six-year-old little girl. I would take off my shoes, get down on my hands and knees, and then lay down and hug that foot log and crawl all the way across to the other bank.

The very thought of this traumatized me. I thought, "What if I was to fall into the creek while crossing? The water could wash me far away, and possibly kill me." I became so afraid of water that it took two people to wash my hair, one to hold me down and the other to wash it.

It was important for us to get to school five minutes before the bell rang so we could get in line. But in the winter, it was almost impossible. We would walk through the snow. By the time we got to school, our feet and hands were so cold that they didn't have any feeling in them. Many times, the cold would make us late. But once we arrived, there was a large potbelly stove that burned wood, and it was what we used to warm ourselves through. You wanna know the truth? If we were late sometime, we got a licking' on the behind. I think about that now. Shame on them! It could've been anything that made us late. If it was bad weather, why would they want to paddle us? They knew nothing else to do, I don't reckon. They didn't ask us why; they just disciplined us. I reckon they figured we were out there playing or something.

We only went to school six months out of a year because when the crops were ready to be gathered and the cotton was ready to be chopped, they would take the children out of school to work the field until the crops were finished. I loved school so much that I was willing to make whatever sacrifice it took for me to go.

My first school was Mc Mittress School. It was a large white building where first grade through twelfth grade went. My principal's name was Mr. Smith. He and his wife both taught at the school. He was a stout man with a hump in back. Frank's teacher was Mrs. Lewis, and I had Mrs. Turner, a slender, tall Negro lady with long hair and a great personality. She was a wonderful teacher who loved her students. Those teachers cared about us so much that when a problem came up, they would go home and even stay the night with our family. Our teachers knew Grandma meant business when it came to education. I was smart as a whip. I did so well in school that I passed two levels in one year; I caught up with Frank, and we ended up in the same grade.

There are things about school I love to remember and things I would rather forget. I know I loved sports when I was a child. I was always trying to play ball after school. My favorites were baseball and basketball. It seemed like the best times of my life were when I got a chance to play those two sports. There was a large basketball court on campus, but I seldom got the chance to play because most of the day was dedicated to our studies. After-school was the only time that we could play, but unfortunately, we couldn't stay after school because Grandpa was strict about us coming straight home once school let out.

The activities were very limited for girls then. It was not very popular for girls to play basketball or baseball. They were to focus on learning how to take care of the home and children. When I expressed interest in a profession, they would always say, "Girls make good nurses, not doctors; good teachers, not principals."

Grades one through five were wonderful. My grandmother supported my teachers in every way she could, and she gave me and my siblings a love that will never leave my heart. Those times are fixed in my memory forever. I believe they have helped me to become who I am today.

TOYS AND CHILDHOOD FRIENDS

From the 1800's to the 1950's, tightly woven cotton sacks were used to hold and carry flour. After the flour was all gone, Momma and my sisters always found things to make with the flour-sack fabric: curtains, towels, tablecloths, books, quilts, aprons, pillowcases, and dresses, and they would be beautiful! Those flour sacks had flowers and other nice prints on them. I remember my very first toy. It was a doll that was drawn on the flour sack. Alee and MaeLee cut out, sewed, and stuffed my baby doll with cotton. The final touch was her hair; they used yarn to make the hair flow long and beautiful. She was my best friend; I would always sleep with her in my arms.

Toys bought from the store were out of the question during those times. Frank and I would make our own soft balls by wrapping rags around a rock, or we would go outside and make mud cakes by mixing water with dirt and put the cakes on a tin pan lid, sit it in the sun, and let it bake. We would then gather leaves pretending to cook greens. We used bucket lids and jar tops for our pots and pans. Then we would top it all off by setting the table, using a board and placing newspaper on top of it. I would dress up in some of my older sister's clothes and play mother of the house, and Frank would be the dad. I seemed to always think of family and having one of my own someday. It was a lot of fun for us.

Frank and I also loved to play outside with our dog, old Henry. He was black and had brown spots. We would take old Henry out and hunt in the woods or just walk up to the spring barefoot where we would get our drinking water for the house. We had well water for washing clothes and taking baths, but it wasn't sufficient to drink. That sparkling spring water was clean and cold as ice. We used the foot tub. I would catch one side, and Frank would catch the other side, and we would bring our drinking water from the spring. They told me that barefoot walking would make my feet wide, but I didn't care!

Frank and I would also take old Henry with us for fishing on those lazy summer days. That was also where I would go to think when things were not going my way. We played other games like hopscotch, hide-and-seek, jacks with a ball, and honey in the bee ball. We made wagons with four large lids and a flat board nailed to the side for a slide, going down the hill. We climbed trees, rode horses, and played tit-a-tat. I was always excited about my cousins coming to see us. It was a treat to see my favorite cousin, Bertha. We always got along well together. All my aunties and uncles had children, but Bertha was special. Our birthdays are exactly eight days apart.

We would go to their house and play stickball. At night we'd get into groups and go out into the woods to view the star-filled sky between those hundred-year-old trees, or we would thrash birds. I should explain this one. When Grandpa Frank would cut down brush to make a turnip patch, he would stack the tree branches in a pile to dry. Those branches would become wood to burn on those cold winter nights. While the pile of brush was drying out, birds would go to the root of the brush to roost. We knew that they were there for the night, so we would get a long-thorn bush and then shake the brush, so the birds would fly out. That's when we would thrash them with the thorns and kill them. We would take them home, scald them in hot water and pick their feathers, clean and cook them over an open fire, and enjoy a good meal. That was some good eating.

As kids, we went to the church where my grandmother worshipped. It was called Dank Town Church of God In Christ (COGIC). Although it was later renamed Washington Chapel, folks from miles around knew it as the "Powerhouse Church" because the Holy Spirit would come in and "slay the house!" This church was part of a larger organization called the Churches of God In Christ, which was founded in 1897 in Memphis, Tennessee, by Charles H. Mason. He was heavily influenced by a Negro Methodist Evangelist who led many people into the Holiness movement. The Church of God In Christ was divinely revealed and inspired by the holy scripture found in 1 Thessalonians 2:14:

> "*For ye, brethren, became followers of the churches of God in Judea which are in Christ Jesus; for ye also have suffered like things from your own countrymen, even as they have from the Jews.*"

This is the church where the Washington's and Glover's got their spiritual heritage. All my aunties and uncles were raised here. The first prayer and Bible band was started by Aunt Addie and my grandmother. Bible band was where young women were taught to carry themselves as upstanding Christians. My uncle Jack Glover pastored this church for as long as I can remember. He was my blood grandpa, Joe Glover's brother.

I would always watch my grandmother's attitude toward other people. She was a wonderful woman. I look back and thank God that I was raised in a Christian home. There were so many things Momma did that I did not understand. She loved to pray and read the Bible. I would watch how she would go without food or water for several days when something came up that she didn't understand. She stood on the scripture for her answers, as it says in Joel 2:12:

> "*Therefore, also now, saith the LORD, turn ye even to me with all your heart, and with fasting, and with weeping, and with mourning.*"

At the end of her fast, she would use an ancient Native Indian recipe to make "pone." She would pour hot water over cornmeal, divide it into small pieces, wrap it in corn shuck, and cover it with coal or ashes from the fireplace, and then let it cook until done. She would eat it and drink black coffee to break her fast. Momma was a woman of great faith. She always said, "If God don't do it, leave it undone. I'm telling' you what I know!"

We needed this kind of faith in our house, especially when malaria hit. Yes, malaria did hit our house, but the power of prayer, fasting, time-tested remedies, and the ninety-first Psalm— *"A thousand shall fall at thy side, and ten thousand at thy right hand; but it shall not come nigh thee"*—healed us. Al and I were gravely ill with malaria fever; it was in the summertime. Momma would pray for us and anoint us with olive oil that had been blessed. She would also break our fever by putting eucalyptus leaves under our sheets and use a polace cloth to keep our bodies cool. The fever got so bad Al began to go into convulsions. But Momma never lost faith. We were sick for several weeks, but we were kept cool, and prayer was being constantly abounded. We were never taken to a doctor for that fever. We were healed from this and other illness throughout our childhood by the power of a praying grandmother. Her faith and discipline were a great help in my walk with God. Being raised by a Baptist father and a Holiness grandmother has given me the most glorious Christian background any child could ever pray for. The experience I had as a child is wealth for me now.

In the 1930s, very few Negroes owned automobiles. They often traveled by horse and covered wagons. My grandmother would travel all over by horse and wagon just to see what God was doing in the saving and healing business. Being a small child, I did not understand then, but I now know and have experienced some of these same healings. God healing me is one of the reasons I wanted to write this book, because my family will never know if I don't reveal it to them. Everything is so different today, and we don't see the same type of healing or miracles today as we did when I was a child.

Back row from left to right: Lillie Mae Hardwell, Artie Bell Jones, Wasika Ferguson, Louvenia Caldwell, Bessie Ferguson, Mattie Glover and Samantha Bank
Front row from left to right: Hazel Hardwell, Addie Doss, Emma Washington, Pauline Murphy and Oshab Washington
(Photo courtesy of Eldema Simms)

Photo courtesy of Emma Simms

The first Bible Band was started at Washington Chapel
by my grandmother, Emma Washington and my aunt Addie

HISTORY OF WASHINGTON CHAPEL

As is illustrated in the picture of an early Washington Chapel prayer band, many of our ancestors were pioneers in the establishment of various churches of God In Christ in Southern Arkansas and Northern Louisiana. Elder Jack "J.C." Glover was a pioneer, establishing numerous churches in Arkansas and Louisiana. Three of those churches were located in Emerson, Arkansas: Washington Chapel, Heard Chapel and Emerson COGIC.

Elder Jack Glover was born in Shongaloo, Louisiana, March 15, 1879 to Grant and Carolyn Glover. He was a man with a purpose and he went out into the highways and hedges helping his fellow man. Elder Glover was often met with persecution in his efforts to bring men and women to Christ. He and many of the earlier pioneers of the church suffered verbal and physical attacks. It was not uncommon to have rocks and knots of wood thrown at the early converts during church services. There are tales of shots being fired at Pastor Glover in an effort to run him off. He believed, when God is in the plan, there is nothing that man can do to alter it. Washington Chapel was originally named, "Dank Town Church of God". With the emergence of Elder Glover, it became Dank Town Church of God In Christ. The state bishop at the time was Bishop Hightower, and the district superintendent was Elder B. I. Whitlow.

The church building soon became too small, so a brush arbor was built to extend the capacity of the church. A brush arbor consists of sticks stuck in the ground with brushes or limps placed on the ground and on the top to protect occupants from the weather. In the 1930's, Mr. Dank Glover, the brother of Jack Glover, donated land to build a new church. In 1938 a new church building was completed. Elder Archie Dean Washington was given the honor of renaming the church because he had been among the group who raised the most money toward the building of the church. The church was named "Washington Chapel COGIC."

The first church built in Emerson was a wood framed church, but in 1953 a stone church was built. Although Elder Glover's health declined, he was determined to build a church in Emerson. Much of the finances for this church came from his personal commitment to this cause. The land on which Glover Memorial now stand was part of the estate of Elder Jack Glover and was donated to the church by his daughter, Mrs. Meaker White, in his memory. Although Elder Glover lived in the State of Louisiana, his religious services spread throughout Arkansas and his contributions continue to make an impact there.

Early members of Dank Town, Washington Chapel and Emerson Churches include: My grandmother, Emma Ferguson, Emma Lee Reliford,

Nolan Ferguson, Archie Dean Washington, Earnest Lindsey, Luther Washington, Clarence Doss, Andrew Ferguson, Albert Ferguson, Ike Thomas, Onnie Maxie, Addie Doss, Oshab Washington, Essie Cooper, Bell Cooper, Pearl Copeland, Mattie Glover, Roberta Thomas, Lillie Mae Hardwell, Lizzie Murphy Fred Reliford, Sue Willie Reliford, Daisy Wheeler, Herman Wheeler, Johnny Reliford, Seland Caldwell.

Elder Jack Glover served as Pastor of Washington Chapel, Heard Chapel and Emerson Churches until 1958. June 18, 1959, He went to be with God. Emerson and Washington Chapel were always sister churches, and in July of 1989 the members of both congregations agreed to consolidate the churches and rename it, "Glover Memorial," in honor of their founding pastor, Pastor Jack Glover.

CHAPTER 2

Living with Papa for Good

(1936-1941)

I Left Momma to Live with Papa

I was only ten years old when I was suddenly pulled away from my grand-mother, finding the freedom to live with Papa and the madness that was also attached to it. The reality of living with Papa was sobering. I was no longer the baby, and frankly, I just didn't feel the way I felt with Momma. I had lived off and on with my dad. When he had someone to take care of me, he would come pick me up and take me to live with him. And when he didn't have anyone to take care of me, he would take me back to my grandmother's place. Being small, I needed supervision. Alee and MaeLee could stay with Papa because he could watch over them. They were old enough to cook and take care of themselves, but they were too young to watch over me, and then again, there was work to be done in the fields. I don't know just how long I had stayed with him before, because it's vague in my mind, but this time it was for good. I didn't want to leave Momma, but I had no choice. Papa came for me, and I had to go.

This all happened after the problems my family had with my best friend's father. There had been some very serious problems with Grandpa Frank and the older man, Jimmy Dean, which was attracted to one of my sisters. Grandpa Frank could be mean as a bull if you crossed him. I was nervous because that old man had done worse than cross Grandpa—he attacked MaeLee! She was so scared that she headed out walking to Papa's after she got attacked. I felt the rage in the house as Grandpa Frank went looking for Jimmy Dean. Next thing we knew, Grandpa was taken to jail because he cut that dirty old man with a jock knife and neh 'bout killed him. That man almost lost his life. He was in the hospital for a long spell. I was so troubled behind this. It made me sad to leave Momma. With Grandpa in jail and all of us gone, she would be left there alone. Grandma's children lived down on the next farm in the same vicin-ity, but I still couldn't imagine how she felt when she found herself alone in an empty nest, but I had no choice in the matter. Papa came and got us younger children: Al, Frank, and I. We moved to Old Shongaloo, Louisiana, to live with Papa for good.

When I arrived at Papa's house, I learned that he was married and had started another family. Not only did I have a new stepmother, Alee, but I also had a one-year-old baby brother, Lonnie Junior, and Ms. Alee had three other boys. She was very ill at the time with the dropsies. It stood out in my mind because I still can visualize how severely swollen her feet were. She couldn't do much, so we all pitched in and kept the house clean and the clothes washed. There was always something to do at this house. With Papa's five children and her three, plus the one that they had together, there were plenty of things to be done. I didn't like this job. I just wanted to play and have fun like I did on the farm. I thought about running away, but I didn't know where to go. Plus, I didn't want to leave my sisters and brothers, so I stayed and endured the pain.

I didn't think of this woman as a mother figure. I was too old and too detached to call her mom, so I just thought of her as "Papa's wife" and treated her the same. I was so unhappy. It was the first time I had been away from my grandmother for good. Of course, I felt invisible. I never got any attention because there were so many other people in the house.

Ms. Alee and Papa didn't stay together very long after I came to live with them. But he was very sensitive and tried to do the right thing. He allowed me to stay with my stepmom and help take care of her and my little brother. I never understood why Papa chose me when she had children of her own. It didn't last for too long. I don't remember whether she passed or what, but Lonnie Junior and I went back home to live with Papa.

We lived for some time without a stepmother, and that was fine with me. But soon after, Papa met and moved with another lady named Jane Wilson. She and her three sons and Papa and his five children made another really big family. So, we moved into a large four-bedroom house with a wide hall between the bedrooms. Al, Junior, and I shared a room. We had lived with so many people and had learned to get along with just about anyone, but we still had problems. Mine began on the first day of school.

Because I loved school, I would get up extra early in the morning to prepare myself. In those days school was not mandatory, it was a luxury. So, I asked Papa about going to school and he said, "Ask Jane." When I asked her she said, "Naw, you can't go nowhere, guh! You got clothes to wash!" I was so hurt because she knew how much I loved school.

From that day forward, it was always something to keep me from going to school. I never understood why she had such a negative view toward education. I now understand that this was part of a mentality that was prevalent in Negroes in that day. This was 1935, during the Great Depression, which doubled for Negroes. Negroes didn't see education as important as domestic and agricultural jobs. W. E. B. Dubois wrote as follows:

> "A separate Negro school where children are treated like human beings, trained by teachers of their own race, who know what it means to be a negro in the year of salvation 1935, is infinitely better than making our boys and girls doormats to be spit and trampled upon and lied to by ignorant social climbers, whose sole claim to superiority is the ability to kick "niggers" when they are down."

My stepmother treated me so unfair. But being raised by them, it simply meant that they had guidelines, and I had to follow them. Thank God W. E. B. Dubois was fighting for my education, because it sure wasn't Ms. Jane.

It was she who caused me to get the worst whippin' of my life. It was just I and Papa. He was so angry that it appeared to me that there was fire in his eyes. He hit me so hard that the skin on my thighs broke and blood began to roll down my legs. I got this one because I went on top of the roof after Papa had told me not to. I was a tomboy and always loved to climb trees and go on top of the roof with my brother. But this time I did it only because Ms. Jane told me to.

I was only obeying my stepmother, but she told Papa half-truths. So, this is what happened: we used to pick our peaches off the tree and peel them, cut them into thin slices, and place them on paper, and then we would lay the paper on the roof and let them stay there until they dried, if it didn't rain. This day, the rain came up suddenly, and Ms. Jane told me to go on top of the house and get those peaches down before they got wet.

Mind you, I had been told by Papa to never climb that high. I was caught between a rock and a hard place. I knew if I didn't obey her, Papa would have whip my behind, so I climbed up and got the peaches. I couldn't trust her because she had betrayed me before. When Papa came home from work, she told him that I climbed on top of the roof. I felt she should have said, "Ozell disobeyed you, but I told her to do it Lonnie." Papa beat me to the edge of my life. I still have the scars to prove it. I shall never forget it.

I began to hate my stepmother because she was so mean to my sisters and me. It was so unfair, the abuse I received from Papa because of her lies. Although Al was there, she was not going on top of that roof; she was too scared of heights. She would have fought that woman before she did. Ms. Jane's sister Amy was there also. Why didn't she ask her? I never understood why she told me to do it. It's been years since that happened, and my blood pressure goes up every time I think about Ms. Jane.

I felt like Papa would do things just to keep the peace. I can imagine that he was on an emotional teeter-totter, attempting to balance the relationship between his kids and Ms. Jane. She would try to move Papa with her threats: "You give me January and February? And I'll march right on out of here!" I don't really think it made Papa no mind. He wasn't moved by her threats. I believe his desire to truly love was buried with Josie on that rainy September day. Papa had an air of apathy that was like a cloud suspended above the earth; those threats floated right by him. Eventually she and Papa split, and she moved within walking distance from our house; we were without a stepmother once again.

Although we didn't live in the same house, Ms. Jane and I still saw one another. In fact, we shared the same vegetable garden. By this time, I was older and almost waiting for her to say something to me. When we got ready for fresh vegetables, we would have to go to the garden that we shared, and she wanted me to still ask her for permission to get our vegetables. Well, I was fed up with how she had treated me, and I rebelled and refused to ask her for anything. I would just go to the garden and get my vegetables. Somehow Ms. Jane never attacked me; she must have seen the hate in my eyes. I am so glad that she didn't say anything, because I was ready for a fight, and that would have caused a huge problem with Papa.

Going Back to Emerson to the Church Meeting

It had been a long time since we had seen my grandmother, so we wanted to go up to Emerson to visit her and go to our home church where they had a big meeting that we called the protracted meeting. It was an annual convention that came once a year in August. They would have a big service, and people would come from far and near. The women would bring large boxes and even trunks of food: goat, chicken, tenderloins, duck, and turkey. Al and I asked Papa to let us go up to see Momma and stay for that Fourth-Sunday celebration after church. He agreed but made it firm: "Be back before sundown Sunday." We left out that Friday walking through the woods for about ten miles to Momma's house.

We spent Saturday with Momma and on Sunday we went to church. We thought church would end in time for us to eat some of the homemade dressing and pound cakes, but it didn't. We had to leave before service ended if we were going to make it home before sundown. That broke our hearts because we were very hungry. But we left anyway. Our timing was obviously off, because it took us longer than we thought, and it became dark before we got home. We took a shortcut through the woods, but it didn't help. Papa thought we purposed to disobey him, so we both got a whipping. I always thought it was enough not being able to see my old friends or have some of that good food. I have never gotten over with that. Good Lord, I just thought my papa was the meanest man on earth because he made guidelines for us.

My Papa the Super Protector

Papa was a super protector with the girls, and I sometimes think he over-protected us. He spent a lot of time teaching us how to act and what our roles were as girls.

Everybody knew my Papa carried a pistol, and he had no problem using it if he had to. I remember there was a single man who would come to the house to visit Papa. And I believe my dad must have told him to stay away from the house when he wasn't home. You see, Papa trusted no one, because he knew what they were after: his girls. One-day Al and I were outside doing laundry, and the man came over and began talking with us. Do you know when Papa came home, he didn't open his mouth; he just went inside the house, got his pistol, came out, and said one word, "*You!*" and commenced to shooting. That man shot out under the fence. If he had not ducked, Papa would have killed him. The law came and picked Papa up, but they didn't keep him. I think they admired him because he was an honest, upstanding man. I used to wonder, "Why did Papa shoot at that man?" Now I know. That man was a friend of my dad's, and he was an older man. He knew better than to make conversation with young girls. He knew Papa didn't take mess off nobody. I don't think that man was expecting my dad to do anything, seeing they were friends and all. But that scared me so bad! I thought, "You mean the man is going to die just for talking to us?" Papa never bothered us or said a word about that situation. I guess one way or another, everybody got the message.

Today, I am so grateful for that strict upbringing. Whereas I used to talk about Papa, over the years I've come to believe that he was a caring father. He had all these kids he could have dumped at somebody's house and got lost. People even asked Papa for us, my uncle wanted to raise us and give us a proper education. But there had to be some care and love on my papa's part because he always said no. When I got grown, I began to look back and understand why my dad went overboard protecting us. He lived his life the way he wanted to, but he intentionally taught us the best he knew how. There were some things my grandmother didn't know about the world. She taught us about God and spirituality, but Papa gave us the practical lessons about street life.

Papa Got Sick with the Ulcers

I was around ten years old when Papa was sick with ulcers. My papa drank, and I think that may have had a bearing on his health. I believe it may have contributed to his ulcer. He lost so much weight. He could not keep any food down; it would just run through him.

Al and Frank were living with my uncle. Papa and I moved to Alee and Cellis' house because he was not able to provide for us now because he needed twenty-four-hour care. I had no choice but to take on the role of an adult. That meant I was to cook food, keep the house, babysit my little niece Christell, and take care of my dad. Whatever had to be done, I did it at ten years old. He stayed in the hospital a good while, waiting for them to find a cure, and when they had done all they could do, they discharged him to die. He was so sick and so small. He was down to ninety pounds.

After they discharged him, he left and went to Shongaloo, and I didn't see him for a good while. I thought he was dead, and when I saw him again he had meat on his bones. I was happy for that. I think he went to his girlfriend's house, and she helped him get well. I shall never forget the hospital that wrote him a letter and told him to come back, that they had found a cure for him, but he was already well.

Since Papa was gone, I stayed with Alee and Cellis, and I continued to help around the house. I remember a time when I was supposed to put on a pot of black-eyed peas so that Cellis would have food at noon when he took his break. I put Christell to sleep, and instead of putting on the peas, I went outside and started playing with my friends. I was having a good time, then all of a sudden, I realized, "hey I forgot to start dinner!" it was close to noon, so I ran back in the house and put the peas on and commenced to playing. Twelve o'clock came, and I saw that furniture truck pull up. Cellis hopped out and ran in the house and went to eating those half-cooked beans. It neh 'bout killed him, he got so sick, but he didn't make a fuss. He was so nice to me, almost like a father.

One of the Saddest Times of My Life

One of the saddest times of my life was when I was about thirteen years old. We lost my nephew, Lonnie Drew, affectionately known as Senior. He was Al's son, but he was like my own. I would wet his hair to comb it into a ponytail. He was my little doll.

We lived across the creek in the bottoms with Papa. One Sunday we were going out in the country to help my stepmom's son gather his crop. We almost ran out of gas while going, because it was Sunday, and all the stations were closed. But somehow, we made it to his house.

On Monday morning everyone went to work. We left Senior in the house with our stepmom while Al, Frank, and I worked in the field. The baby was already sick when we left home, but we thought that everything would be all right. Mrs. Viola, whom we called Ms. Bide, was cooking up dinner and somehow or another fed Senior some raw radish. Minutes later she hollered out, "Y'all come here! Y'all come here! Sum-um done happen ta the baby! Lordy mercy, sum-um done happen ta the baby!" We hightailed it from the fields, chucking the wide bamboo hats that shaded us from the sun into the wind. Once inside we witnessed Senior struggling and gasping for breath, holding his stomach. His little body was going into convulsions, and he was vomiting.

Al cried, "Senior! Ms. Bide, what happened to my baby? What happened to my baby?" "Senior!" she screamed. "Please, baby, talk to Momma!"

Ms. Bide really didn't know that he had a bad stomach (but we did), and she gave him some radish to eat, and it just set his bowels off. He stayed with the runs, and we couldn't stop it. We couldn't take him to a hospital because we were way out in the country. We didn't know anything to do but wrap Senior up and take him to Papa. He always seemed to know what to do. We piled into that old Ford and headed toward Papa's house. The car was moving so slowly. It didn't seem to want to move fast. In every town that we went through, we asked for a doctor, but there was none. We didn't have ice, so we used a wet polace cloth to keep him as cool as possible.

We sat in silence as our bodies rocked back and forth to the rhythm of that old bumpy road. With every mile that drew us closer to Papa's house, Senior's spirit drifted further away. His eyes sunk deep into his face and became dim. With each passing mile, our panic became more of a reality that Senior was leaving us. His body was hot as coal. We shaded him and put a cool cloth on his sweaty body. Al tapped his hand and said, "Senior, stay 'wake. You got a momma that love you and can't let you go. You just three years old. God, you just three years old. Senior, hang on, baby, till we get to Papa. Everything will be just fine."

Oh, I needed to hold him. I told Al, "Give me Senior. Le-le-let me put him in my arms." She passed him to me. I held him close to my heart and cried along with him. Al was crying with a deep sense of her baby being torn away from her. This was a feeling that only a mother knows; the feeling that she is about to lose her child. Al could not stand to watch the life leave her baby's body, so she turned her head and sobbed because the child she birthed into the world was on his way out.

I remember feeling the life leaving his body. I had him in my lap. I knew it because he was boiling hot from fever, and his breathing began to shallow. Suddenly, I felt his body go cold. It sent a chill throughout every cell in my body. His limp body lay there in my arms. I knew that Senior was gone.

I said, "Ms. Bide, something happened to Senior."

She said, "Give him here!" I believe she knew he was dead.

Al screamed out a death cry to the heavens: "My baby is gone! Lord, take me with him. I can't live without him." We sat, numb with grief, as

Senior returned to heaven. We were speechless, because there were no words that were going to bring him back. The fear rang out as I took his small, tender face into the palms of my trembling hands, kissed his fore-head, and said good-bye.

We had a time getting back, but eventually we got him to Papa's, and he carried him into Haynesville to Norton's funeral home. They embalmed him and brought him back to the house. Senior was left in the front room. He stayed with us overnight. We could see him all night, and then we buried him the next day. It didn't seem fair for a coffin to be made so small. I cried all night. I loved that baby. He seemed more like mine than he did Al's. None of us wanted to give Senior up to the grave or accept that he was indeed dead. Some things happen in your life that are devastating, and you won't soon forget them. That dreadful experience haunts me to this day.

CHAPTER 3

Meeting and Marrying A. D.

(1941-1949)

Meeting A.D.

In Psalm 23:2, the Bible speaks of green pastures. There really was such a place when I was growing up. My memory takes me back to the lush carpet of grass that filled the pasture. It stretched as far as my eyes could see, and the scent of honeysuckle put me in the mind of hard candy.

It was on a holiday called Juneteenth that I would see all my friends. I didn't realize it then, but I now know that Juneteenth (June 19, 1865) was the unofficial date that Negroes in America were freed from slavery. I say unofficial because they were freed two and a half years earlier, on January 1, 1863. The news just took that long to get from Congress to the cotton fields. The plantation owners were blamed for waiting to tell the slaves. They were accused of holding back the information until one last cotton harvest was gathered. So, we considered Juneteenth our Independence Day, not the 4th of July. I simply knew it was a day for good food and a lot of fun.

Everyone would gather. They would choose a pasture because it was clean and, most of the time, it was near a spring. We used that spring for our cool drinking water. It was a day for families to gather. Folks would pack their wagon full of food and come from miles around. It seemed to me there would be more than a hundred-people showing up. I don't know; I just remember it was lots of families.

We didn't want to ride on the horse and wagon going. Al, Frank, and I would get a kick out of walking there. You see, if we walked, then our friends could go and come back with us. So that day we walked. We had so much fun picking up our friends along the way, going from one family to another tasting all the different foods. Everybody had cooking going on at their house, but we knew who could cook and who couldn't! Then sometimes folks would have stands along the road with lots of things we enjoyed, like cold drinks and even homemade ice cream. People would come together in love, and there was so much culture there. One person didn't try to make him or herself better than the other. You could mix with anybody.

I enjoyed it because I got to meet so many different people from all the little country towns surrounding Shongaloo. With all of them woods you couldn't tell it but nestled in between the trees were big communities of people. The later it got, the more people would emerge from seemingly nowhere. Now that's the truth! It started around twelve noon, but by four in the afternoon people started swarming in.

When I smelled the scent of that goat on the barbie, I knew it was a sign that a feast was in store. There was enough food to celebrate all day and even throughout the weekend—and sometimes it would last just that long! The women laughed and talked as they filled the tables up with large butter pound cakes, sweet potato pies, egg custard, fresh cornbread dressing, and tubs filled with greens. The men congregated and spoke of hunting as they placed their prize-winning hogs, billy goats, and ducks on the barbie. There was enough food and cold drinks for anyone who came.

But the food was just the beginning. Hands clapped, and feet stomped to the tune of one person picking the guitar or another playing the harmonica. Others played dominoes and cards. Some played baseball while others sat on the sidelines, yelling, "Come on, make your base!" Can you imagine all those folks coming together and enjoying good, clean fun—no killing or fighting with one another? It was all about love, being with our neighbors, and finding ways to make our lives richer and fuller. We didn't have a lot of money, but we did have that. We seemed to love one another all the more after those gatherings. That was what life was all about in those days. Those gatherings were also the place where girls and boys would come together to get to know one another, maybe even start courting.

Getting to Know A. D.

It was at Juneteenth where A. D. saw me. I had known him for some time—since he was about thirteen years old. He used to pick up work around town. You see, his mother was just a kid when he was born, and since that was her only child, she was easy going when it came to him. She didn't have a tight ring on him the way Papa did on us. He was raised most of the time by his grandparents, Louise (Lou) and Smiley Miller. After Mr. Smiley died, he and his grandmother lived from here to there—with aunties, cousins, and kids. He said that Ms. Lou used to walk barefoot everywhere she went; heat, rain, or snow, it didn't mat-ter. Then, one winter she caught the three-day pneumonia and just died. He was nine years old when that happened, and that's when he began to pick up work on his own.

A. D. hired himself out for wages at the next farm over from us. I remember him whistling and singing and carrying on while he worked. You could hear him clear across the field! He was just showing off and wanted me to see him. I didn't pay him no mind; I just kept chopping my cotton. We always knew him as "the grown little boy across the fence." He had a nice wildness about him. He seemed fearless, and he was comfort-able with that fearlessness. I could tell laughs came to him easy. But he also had a reputation for being a hothead, and he would say what came to his mind—white folks, black folks, it didn't matter. I always thought, "That boy's going to get hurt someday, talking to white folks that way!"

When I think back, he had such fair skin that they may have mistook him for one of their own.

Papa knew his mother, Mrs. Ella Mae, a good while. She was a well-dressed woman who wore a skirt, heels, stock-ings, earrings, and beads just to do house chores—but that was Ms. Ella Mae. She was married to Mr. Joe Robinson, a farmer by day and performed on the chit-terling circuit by night. He was in a group that made a 78 record, and they would sing all over. They stayed on the next hill

A.D. at sixteen

from us. They were one of the only families at that time who had a car. It was a Model A Ford, probably about a 1936, and that's how we knew them: "Ah, ta ta ta ta ta…ta ta tahhhh, ta ta ta ta." You could hear that car coming from way down the road.

A. D. and I had never thought about corresponding, but that day at Juneteenth, it was different. After my siblings and I walked around half the day, we got tired and were ready to go. That's when A. D. asked if he could walk me home. Just then, his girl—I reckon it was his girl—found out, and she was ready to whip me good!

I told him, "There your girlfriend is. She's clowning me, and you asking to walk with me?"

He said, "Yeah!"

And we turned, walked away, and left her standing there. I think she had a knife, but that didn't frighten me. I didn't want to fight her, but not because I was afraid; I just didn't want to face Papa after I had knocked the daylight out of her. He always had high morals for us, and he would have almost killed me if he thought I was out there fighting over a boy—I knew that! I knew better than to scrap with her over A. D. I just thought, "If he wants you, y'all can go on. It doesn't bother me," but he insisted that wasn't his girl. And that was my first time meeting him on a one-on-one basis.

The Walk Home

I don't remember how far the walk back home was, but it sure seemed a lot farther going back than it did coming! I sometimes struggle to remember all the details, but I can remember how much fun it was for us young people walking together. I can still smell red-clay dirt in the breeze. We crossed perfect creeks and streams and made fun about how the pastor had been seduced into a deep sleep by the midday sun. Oh! I wanted those walks to last forever because they made me feel so free. We were kids of the same age, and we entertained each other the entire way home.

Isn't it funny? We took all that beautiful nature for granted. We were not entranced by the sun that peeked through those sweet gum trees, nor were we enchanted by the gentle winds that tossed those tall pine trees all around us. We weren't amazed by the birds that sang in harmony with nature. And we didn't think twice about how the same woods that made us feel so free could be very dangerous if the wrong people found us there! Oh, if only the woods could reveal its secrets. We were just a group of curious kids making our way home; it was second nature to us. We knew our way like hound dogs. The maze was seared in our teenage minds. We exited the woods, and as dust that was kicked up from the passing horse and buggy began to settle on the country road, we could see just over the horizon, the sun beginning to set on Papa's farm. This was a sure sign that our lazy day was over. It was also the beginning of a spark between A. D. and me.

Later that summer the neighborhood church, White Rose Baptist had a box lunch supper. We had lots of fun playing penny march; I should explain. We were to march around the auditorium, and every time you reached the table, you had to drop a penny in the bucket. If a boy likes you, he would put a penny in for you as well. Girls and boys did not see one another often, so special occasions like this were when we could really enjoy one another.

All us kids went to the social, and A. D. stayed in my face all while we were there. But I had another friend there with me. We had been corresponding for about a year, and I had grown very fond of him. That night a girl did the same thing to me with the boy I really thought I was in love with and had planned to marry, that the girl at the Juneteenth celebration did to me over A.D. My friend was fixin' to take me home, and a girl confronted me and took his hand away from me and said, "You takin' me home!" What puzzled me was that he turned around right then and left with her. Again, a confrontation would have gotten me in trouble with Papa; he just didn't believe in that. Because somebody was sure going to tell him, "You know what? Ozell and that girl was fighting over that boy!"

That would have been it for me, and I knew it. So, what did I do to stay out of trouble? I kept my peace. Those girls were something else. I later learned that he married her too! After A.D. and I were married, I asked my ex-friend, "Why did you do that? Y'all weren't even close like me and you." We had been close for a year. We lived across the creek from one another, and he had come to my house—we had even made plans to marry. I just didn't understand it. I don't remember what he told me. I'm sure it was a good story, but anyhow, that's water under the bridge.

A. D. saw how that other boy treated me, and that was just as good as he wanted. He came over and asked me again, "Well, can I walk you home?" I said, "If you want to, I suppose it's fine with me," and he walked me home that night. That walk home was when we started seriously corresponding.

We started going to school and church functions throughout the summer. It had to be something morally good for Papa to say yes. But I've never heard the last of A. D. saying, "Ozell, you took me on the rebound." He made his own story up. I told him, "I'm not going to lie...I thought a load of that kid who just picked up and left with that other girl. Of course, I was just a kid myself."

Our relationship was solidified. He would come over to the house, and we went to courting. A.D. was something else! I remember one time he came over, and we were in the front room. Papa was in the front room too because that's where he slept. He had the nerve to reach over and ask me for a kiss—right there! Papa was asleep just a few yards away in the same room. Boy, I'm telling you, he knew what he wanted and just went for it!

The engagement did not even last a year, when A. D. asked me to marry him, and I told him, "I reckon so." When Ms. Rosie Bell and other white folks found out about our engagement, they said, "No! Not to him. That's one of Mr. Lonnie's girls!" They knew my reputation for being nailed down and his reputation for being bold and streetwise. We planned to marry anyway, he always said it was love at first sight.

It had gotten in the wind that Al was going to marry a man named Clinton. I didn't want to be at home without her, and she didn't want to leave me there.

She told me, "Ozell, I ain't gone leave you here by yourself, but I'm gettin' married."

So, I got busy planning for my own wedding.

The Wedding

On January 19, 1942, exactly six months from our first walk home on Juneteenth, my wedding day finally came. I had on a beautiful dress that I had ordered from Waterfield's catalog. Everything was ready; the starting time came and passed, and A. D. was nowhere to be found. I thought, "Maybe he changed his mind?" After about an hour, I saw A. D. coming down that long, narrow country road with a box in his hand. His mom had washed and packed all his clothes for him. He was taking his time as usual, walking slowly. I was almost having second thoughts, but we carried on with the ceremony anyway. When I think back, I recall that his uncle Edgar was the only one from his side of the family who came to the wedding. Neither his mom, Mr. Joe, nor anybody else came. I never understood why.

The marriage was private—A.D.'s uncle Edgar, Papa and his friend Yancy Williams. Papa and Yancy signed the marriage certificate. Getting married was a new reality for both A. D. and me. I had jumped the broom from childhood into adulthood, and what Reverend Goodman, the pastor of White Rose had me say kept ringing in my head: "Till death do us part." I made a vow to God, and I had every intention on keeping it. We were always taught that marriage was very sacred, and you don't abandon it at the first sign of trouble.

There was never a honeymoon, but we were determined to make our marriage work. It helped that we first became friends who honored, respected, and encouraged one another, but there were times when I didn't understand what I had done. We were so young to make such a big commitment.

When A. D. joined my family, I knew he wasn't going to ever leave it. He loved my family, and everybody loved him. My papa treated him like as son; they would exchange corny jokes. Alee and MaeLee loved him, and my uncles and aunties loved him. One of my aunties would always joke with him by saying, "Come here, you little short thang!" He would respond, "I bet I'm taller than you!" They had fun together. He always treated my family with great respect.

AFTER THE WEDDING

After the wedding, A. D. moved in with me, Papa, Lonnie Jr., and Al in Old Shongaloo. Frank had already married, and he and his wife lived in Shongaloo. Alee and MaeLee were married and living in other towns. It was very hard to adjust, but we both tried to commit to our vows. I was raised in a Christian home that taught "till death do you part," so it was a lifetime commitment as far as Grandma and Papa was concerned. Like any young couple, we had many obstacles to overcome, and sometimes it seemed like the marriage would not survive the storms.

Getting Pregnant with Urie

Within the first year, I got pregnant with Urie. This was again something I had no knowledge of; I was just a teen. I was lonely and unhappy because my family was gone. Al got married and Papa decided to get out of the farming business. And in those days, when you stopped sharecropping, you had to leave the farm. So, he and Lonnie Jr. moved away, but A. D.'s folks lived close—thank God for that. They were some of the nicest people I ever met. The doctor took me off my feet because I started to bleed and almost miscarried. A. D. and I were young, and we went back and forth fussing and fighting and I almost lost our son as a result. I shall never forget how A. D.'s cousin, Everett, came and took care of me while I was on bed rest. "Ozell," he would say, "don't you do nothing!" I believe God put him and A. D.'s other cousin, Rosa Lee, in my life to help finish raising and encouraging me. I was just a kid. I tell you, it was a rocky road, but A. D.'s folks helped us out. Those people genuinely loved me; they were so sweet.

While I was still pregnant, Alee came to the country to stay with us awhile. It must have gotten in the wind that something was going on. She told me, "Ozell, I want you to come home with me so that you can have that baby in a hospital." She gave me the information on how I could go to Shreveport Charity Hospital to give birth to our baby. Bless her heart, that's why I love her so. We left and went to Shreveport to stay with her and Cellis until the baby was due.

When it was time, A. D. rushed me to the hospital. My blood pressure was so high it's a wonder I didn't die. They said I had eclampsia, a toxic condition caused by extremely high blood pressure in pregnant women. Of course, I had no knowledge of this because I had no prenatal care out there in the country. I couldn't deliver in the regular ward because the baby and I were both in danger. So, A. D. rolled me into the emergency toxemia unit, and I had to go in labor alone. Thank God, He put that on Alee's heart to come and get me. I was blessed to be in a hospital, because if I were in the country, I may have lost my baby, or worse, I may have lost my life!

I was used to babies being born in the country by midwives. It was usually someone your family knew. In the hospital they treated you different, and I didn't like that. In those days white people would talk to you like you had a tail. If it wasn't "gal," it was "ainie." If you were male, they would call you "boy" or "uncle." Even little kids would call you that! So, it would sound like this, "Okay, gal, puuuush!" White people simply had no respect for Negro folks.

BACK TO THE COUNTRY

After Urie was born, we returned to the country. There was not a house within miles of us, but we stayed there to take care of our child. The farm gave us plenty of time to be with one another as a young family. Our first child was so precious to us. I walked around with him on my hips all the time. We were young and inexperienced, but our baby seemed to have brought us closer together at that time.

A. D. went and hired to a man named Mr. Wiley in the bottoms. We called it Wiley Bottom. There were just two families who sharecropped on the Wiley farm: we had one side of the land, and Ellic Murray had the other.[3]

I was helping A. D. chop peanuts, all while I took care of Urie. I remember how I used a large box for a playpen for the baby while I worked in the field. I would carry him up to the end of the row where I could see him. I would then go back and chop the row up to him. Then I would go to

---

3 *Sharecropping is a system of agriculture in which landowners allow tenants to use the land in return for a share of the crops produced on their portion of land. Sharecropping has a long history, and there is a wide range of different situations and types of agreements that have used a form of the system.*

the next row and do the same thing; I did that all-day long. I was told to be careful because snakes loved breast milk, and they would choke your baby to get the milk. One day I saw a snake headed toward Urie, and I hit it and buried it in the dirt to protect my child. The memory makes me afraid right now! From that point on, A. D. said, "You stay in." He told me, "I'm not gone have you out there with that baby chopping peanuts in the hot sun." So, I went to the cow pen to milk the cows. Here I go, carrying my baby right along with me. I would put him in a wood crate with plenty of quilts all around to keep him warm when it was cold. Nothing stopped us from taking good care of our son.

Mr. Wiley was hiring people to harvest peanuts, and Ellic was trading hogs in exchange for help. A. D. did neither! He was supposed to have somebody out there helping him get the grass out of the peanuts, but because he had taken me and Urie out of the sun, he went and got him a plow—we called it a middle buster—and a horse, and he wrapped those peanuts up. He didn't care what the man said about how he was to harvest them, and the man didn't bother him either. I reckon he said to himself, "This boy don't know what he's doing." A. D. didn't get anybody to get the grass out of the peanuts, he just wrapped them up, and it must have been the best thing that happened to them, because I tell you, you talking about peanuts? I never saw so many peanuts! We had so many peanuts that we didn't know what to do with them. We had enough to give away. It was the special way in which A. D. harvested them that made them come up that way. Only half was ours because we traded the other half with Mr. Wiley. We laughed about that for years.

After one-year A. D. decided we would move back to Shreveport. He felt like the city would give us more opportunity to make a decent living. I will never forget it, we cleared $252 for the year; that was pretty good. In the country, we ate from the land and had a place to stay. So, we took that money and moved back to Shreveport to start our lives there.

Walked the Pipelines

We were trying to make our marriage work. With us being very young and having no experience, it was not easy. Sometimes I felt it was not worth the trials, but I would always look at my baby and remember that his future was the most important thing to both of us. Sometimes I thought it would have been better if we had waited until we were older. The responsibility was almost too much for two young people with a small baby; it caused the marriage to get in serious trouble sometimes.

While we were yet living in the country, we would walk to the small country town to visit Ms. Ella Mae and Mr. Joe on weekends. I remember one occasion when A. D. and I got misplaced from one another, and I walked home alone through the dark woods with Urie on my hip. We were at the house with Ms. Ella Mae and Mr. Joe. A. D. went out with his friends, but he told me to wait for him at the edge of town until sundown, so we could walk home together. Later that day I went where he said we would meet, and I waited for him. I waited until way over in the night, but we never connected, so I started out walking home with my baby. I walked through the woods where snakes, foxes, coyotes, and all kinds of wild animals were loose; I could hear them. It was terrifying to think about how dangerous it was to walk alone at that time of night.

What saved my life was I walked the pipeline. These were exposed pipes that were placed deep into the earth because they were drilling and working in the woods. There were no trails or anything. If it was not for the pipes, I would not have made it, because the woods were impossible to navigate at that time of the night. Plus, my unfamiliar steps would have sent out the sound of my feet crunching leaves and breaking branches on the floor of the woods. I was afraid that my steps would signal the wild animals that I was there. The pipeline gave me steady footing. It must have been about three miles of deep, dark woods. I couldn't see my way; I couldn't even see my hand in front of my face. Every now and then, the wind would blow the branches of the trees, and the moonlight would peek in and shine just enough light, so I could see my way to keep going. When I got home, it was about midnight. I went in and got Urie to bed, but I was so cold my body was numb, I couldn't sleep the rest of the night. I look back and think, "I would have waited all night in town," because A. D. didn't come home until the next morning. I never said anything about it to him until years later. I told him, "I waited for you there at the edge of town, and eventually I walked the pipeline home in the dark woods." He said, "I'm so sorry Ozell, I'm so sorry." I never shall forget it. That is one of my worst horror stories.

Ozell and Al Living Together

It was 1944, and the energy of city was bustling. We came with great anticipation to raise our child. Eat shops and automobiles were everywhere. I got a job at a very fancy, upscale restaurant called Perry Ave Grill on Murphy and Park Avenue. I worked there because I could walk to work. Al and I lived at 1224 Park, so the grill was just a couple of blocks over the hill. I worked at night, so I was home at day with my baby. Al had Cleon and I had Urie, so we shared a one-bedroom house together. It was best because A. D. was working in Houston, Texas, and Clinton was away in the service. When Al would go see Clinton, I kept Cleon, and when I would do something, she kept Urie.

Got Pregnant with Gloria

I soon got pregnant with my second baby. A. D. was still out of town working, so Alee helped us find a place of our own. We had to have a house because we were going to have two children, and we couldn't live in a one-bedroom house anymore. We got a two-bedroom house at 1846 Maple Street. I could always count on my sister Alee and my brother-in-law Cellis. She always gave me the right advice when I had problems with my marriage. It was good to have her stay close by since my husband and I were separated for such long periods of time. She taught me how to keep my family together while he was away.

I made it through another pregnancy, and my second child, Gloria, was born. She was such a small baby. When she started to walk, people were amazed that she looked too small to walk. When her daddy came into town, we would often take her to the silent picture show. We were very young, not even out of our teens. But we were yet trying to adjust for our children's sake.

Soon after, I got pregnant with Arthur, and we moved to 1012 Allen Avenue. A. D. was yet away in Houston. I was working in Shreveport to keep the house going. I worked in a tile factory, cleaned houses, waited tables, anything I needed to do to keep things going. Arthur was a premature baby, he was what we called, an eight-month child.

My Encounter with Racism

Negro folks didn't have any protection in the South. It seemed as if we could be talked to and treated any old kind of way. A. D. was up in Spring Hill with his momma and Mr. Joe; he was looking for work. He had been off in Houston looking for work but came home empty handed. My brother Frank lived across the road from Ms. Ella Mae, and I was up there helping Frank out with his child because his wife was not mentally able to. I often walked across the road to visit Ms. Ella Mae. Gloria and Frank's daughter, Rosemary, were both about two years old, and they were outside playing together. I didn't realize that Rosemary walked across the road on her own to visit Grandma Ella, like she had seen me do so often. This was not a back road in the country; it was a major street that was busy with cars, stores and people moving about.

I was so frightened when she did that, I broke off a little piece of a switch from a tree and just netled (lightly hit) her leg. I explained to her that a car could drive by, hit her, and kill her. That was the only way I knew to let her know how dangerous that was. Just then, out of nowhere a round faced, white bearded lawman came up to me, with dusty boots and tobacco-stained teeth he snatched that switch right out my hand. He told me, "Leave that young'un be!" He was so angry with me. He said, "I'm gone show you how it feels," and hit me with it! I was so startled that it left me speechless. I felt the sting of the switch on my skin, but the anger penetrated much deeper. I thought, "He had his nerve hitting me," but I dare not utter a word. It wasn't so much that I was hurt, I was simply startled that he had the nerve to do that. My first mind said, "Hit him back!" but I had to remember the consequences of the Jim Crow South. That hit would have changed the course of my entire life forever.

I was so mad, I could not wait to tell A. D. and Frank what happened. Frank got so upset that his blood pressure rose. They went to confront the police officer, and he apologized. They obviously approached him in a somewhat respectful manner, because if they had begun to fight the law, they would have been killed on the spot! The next thing you know you would hear, "A. D. and Frank's dead!" It's a shame, but they would have taken them to the morgue and nobody would have thought a thing about it. That's all I have to say about that!

THINKING OF SEPARATING

I don't want to make the mistake of romanticizing marriage. The reality was, I already had two children and was pregnant with my third, and I was barely out of my teens. Motherhood had come up on me faster than

I expected. Although I loved my kids, it was more than I knew how to do, balancing a husband and children.

We were new to what we called the big city, and the shifty ways of some of the people who lived there. Shreveport was full of juke joints; men ate fried baloney sandwiches and drank moonshine, and wild women smoked cigarettes and danced the boogie-woogie to Louis Jordan's latest hit, "Caledonia."

A. D.'s friend from Homer, Louisiana, would come often, pick A. D. up, and they would go out drinking and gambling. A. D. loved to have them over to the house all through the night. Sometimes I didn't say a word, but other times I would put my foot down. Some would make the comment, "She don't look to be that old, but she got all those circles around her eyes." I was tired from taking care of my kids, while A. D. was off making a living; I reckon he was working. He would be gone weeks at a time.

A. D. AT THE CLUB

Don't get me wrong, although I didn't hang out, it didn't mean that I couldn't get on that level. I wasn't afraid of anybody. Don't mess with me! I talked loud and cursed like a sage hen, and I would fight anybody who thought they were bad enough. My big talk mixed with his hothead was a combination for disaster. I would jump on him if he got me that mad. We were just kids. I wasn't even nineteen years old, and I already had two children and had long ago erased the lines between childhood and parenthood.

The juke joint was a couple of doors from Ms. Ella Mae's and Frank's house. I even knew the lady who owned the joint. I once had a feeling that A. D. was there having fun when he was supposed to be at work, so I followed my instincts. Urie, Gloria, and I were at Frank's house at the time, I was pregnant with Arthur. I had moved up to Springhill to help him with his daughter while he worked. Ms. Ella Mae stayed across the street from Frank, so she was able to help me out with my kids. One night I asked her to keep them while I went out. It was raining that night. I went to the juke joint where I knew he hung out. Just as I walked up, I saw that the club was empty, but there was a carload of people out front ready to go off to an after party in another little town. A. D. was there in the front seat with this worldly woman sitting on his lap. I bent over and picked up the biggest brick my hand could hold. Standing there in the driving rain, I looked through A.D.'s eyes, into the deepest part of his soul, then stepped in front of the car, demanding him to stop. I promised to throw that brick through the windshield if he didn't. The anger rose to my throat, and I shouted out, "Get out of the car!" I was so mad. I believe if I had a shotgun, I would have fired it off! Everyone got out the car because they did not want that brick coming through the windshield. They stood there while A.D. and I had it out. All a sudden my upbringing kicked in, and I got shame. My tears melted into the rain, and those times of rejection from my childhood began to creep in through the back door of my mind. I thought, "If my husband didn't care, who would?" I sniffled into my sleeves, turned around, and walked back to Ms. Ella Mae's house.

That woman on my husband's lap took a chance on her life that night. You could fool with another woman's man if you wanted to in those days; there could be severe consequences if it was the wrong woman. Rumor had it that they would take a strand of your hair and have you climbing the walls not knowing why. My cousin got caught up in some crazy mess like that. She went with married man, and when his wife found out, she poisoned my niece. Yep, killed that girl graveyard dead. We couldn't prove it, but that's what was told. My auntie never was quite the same after that.

I turned that thing over in my mind all night long. I was so angry. Thinking A. D. was one place when he was in another was hurtful; I felt so ashamed. Throughout the night, raw tears and raw emotions interrupted my sleep. Why had I cut up over him like that at that club? My tears of anger began to turn to sorrow; it seemed as if I had thrown a lifetime of Christian teaching right out the window. I'd left the safety of Papa's house only to find myself miles away from home, sitting on the edge of my own emotions. I cried myself into a deep sleep, and I awoke the next morning numb. That took something out of me I didn't know I had left to give. My big talk and his short temper? I thought, "Ah, away with that! Let me get out of here." I told Ms. Ella Mae, "I'm going home, and I'm not ever coming back" and you better believe that's just what I did. I packed up my kids up and went back home to 1012 Allen Avenue, in Shreveport, and to this day, I have never been back to Spring Hill.

After a couple of days, A. D. came home, but I didn't pay him no mind because I was fed up with that foolishness. I realized it wasn't so much him I was mad at. It was my own unresolved emotions that were chasing me down. He went back to Houston, and I went back to my normal routine: Working to take care of my three children, cleaning my house, and listening to my favorite song, "Old Buttermilk Sky," on the 4:00 radio program, *In the Groove*.

CHAPTER 4

Learning the Definition of Commitment

(1949-1962)

Definition of Commitment

Webster's definition ~Commitment \kə-'mit-mənt\ com·mit·ment noun, a promise to be loyal to someone or something

Ozell's definition ~I find something or someone worth committing to and use my God-given discipline to carry it out to the end; my marriage and family was what I found.

Joining the Baptist Church

We only had Urie, Gloria, and Arthur at that time. Those three were our life. We had it all planned out. We were determined to only have three, but we were not in God at the time, so our plans were made from our own will and understanding.

I was committed to raising my children in high society. I had great plans to educate them to the best of my knowledge about Baptist ways. I had been influenced by the Baptist church because Papa was Baptist. Although his name was on the roll at White Rose, he seldom went. He didn't feel like he could stick with the ways of holiness. I remember him saying, "Ozell, I can't," and I would tell him, "Yes you can, Papa." But he surely had Baptist values.

So, in my late teens, my good friend Alice Turner encouraged me to join one of the biggest churches in Shreveport, Trinity Baptist. She was an usher there at the time. Oh, how I enjoyed the time I went! Negro doctors wore tailor-made suits, and teachers had fine dresses draped on their backs. It wasn't hard to see myself fitting in because I was very social. In fact, A. D. and I would go with Alice and her husband Floyd to social clubs and dance the Charleston and listen to music like Louis Jordan's "Ain't That Just like a Woman." The men would drink and smoke. I don't know about Alice, but I tried drinking once, and decided I didn't want anything that made me feel that good, so I stopped that mess. Plus, my daddy drank. He wasn't what you would call a drunk, but he would drink socially.

I was getting into a category to socialize and raise my kids in high society. We had the world in a jug and the stopper in our hand! We would have a great time rubbing shoulders with the elite. You know? I figured if I had friends in high society, my children would see positive influences, and that would encourage them to climb the social ladder; I might as well tell the truth. My desire was to raise them where they would be self-sufficient—that was exactly the way I was thinking, which wasn't a bad idea! I wanted my kids to touch the lives of people around them. But at that time, I was looking on a high social level rather than spiritual one. I was anything but spiritual at that time, so when I joined church, all I did was go. I had planned on joining the ushers' board, but I never got involved.

Joining the Holiness Church

My sister Alee went to Looney Street Church of God in Christ, and one day she asked me, "Ozell, we're having a revival at my church. Will you come with me?" I was yet attending Trinity, but I gladly said yes. It was June of 1949. I shall never forget! I sat there and listened to her pastor Superintendent B. T. Kirkpatrick preach, which started out to be a normal sermon. But it looked like the Spirit of God began to "take hold," and that man preached; I mean he preached until his clothes were soaking wet! It seemed as if water was running all down into his shoes. I can see it now! I sat and heard the gospel in full, and the power of God's word convicted me of my sins and showed me my shortcomings. I just had a change of heart. I came under conviction and began to feel very sorrowful.

Thinking back, I will never forget the love that I had for the Baptist church. I yet have a great respect for it to this day. Being a part of it helped me through my teen years and prepared me for marriage and motherhood, but I hadn't felt this way in the Baptist church, because I never accepted Christ in the Baptist church; I should have, but I didn't. It wasn't their fault, it was mine. But that very night, at Looney Street Church of God In Christ, 1800 Looney Street in Shreveport, Louisiana, I was saved. When the pastor made the altar call, I just went! I never once refused prayer, never. So, it was easy to go to the altar because I felt like I was home, like that was where I should have always been.

The next day I went back and told A. D. first, and then I told Alice how God had saved me. Alice said, "Oh-oh, you can't wear nothing but black and white now!" I said it to her then, and I lived it all these almost seventy years, "Oh yes I can. I can wear anything I want to wear!" If I didn't wear something, it wasn't because I couldn't; it was because I didn't want to.

Naturally I stopped going to Trinity, but I also stopped going to Looney Street as well. I stopped because somewhere down in my heart, I felt a whole lot of pride rising. The night of the revival, I was knocked out under the Holy Spirit; it slayed me to the floor. I had on a taffeta sleeve-less dress with a silk organza jacket on top. After I came out from under the Spirit, that top was torn up, and that embarrassed me. I was just over-come with pride. Oh, God, thank you for getting that pride out of me!

Just the thought of me, a dignified woman, on the floor being slayed by the Spirit, tearing my clothes off. I was ashamed! I wasn't just lying down there. I was rolling all over the floor. They had to pick me up and put some-thing around me. The way the dress was made, you could see through the silk organza, and they would make taffeta slips that went under it. Most people don't know anything about that, but in those days, that's what peo-ple wore. When I finally came to myself, the devil said to me, "Do you see what a big fool you made of yourself down there? A dignified woman like you carrying on among all of those people?" And I began to feed on that.

So out of embarrassment, I went home, and I didn't go back. After I missed a couple of weeks, Alee came over and said, "Ozell, I have been missing you. What happened?" I was honest with her; I always could be. I told her that I was embarrassed and felt like I had embarrassed everyone else, although I found out later that it wasn't me, it was the Holy Spirit. And I said to her, "Alee, I don't think I'm saved." Isn't that something? I was letting the devil plant that in my mind. She asked me, "Do you have the same sinful desires? Do you do the same things you were doing before God saved you?" And in my mind, I began to think back over the life I had lived.

"I was full of pride, and I felt like I had done a lot of damage where Ms. Ella Mae lived. A.D. and I would have it out, and I would leave because I thought his mother held against me the fact that her son and I were not getting along. I would think, "She don't want me around here anyway. I'm messing with her son."

I have always been straightforward and surefooted, but it hasn't always been in the right way—and today I'm almost embarrassed to admit that about myself. At times I defied all the home training that Momma and Papa put in me. But because of how I was raised, I always felt like I had to defend myself. After my sisters married and left home, I didn't have that same secure feeling that I had when they lived at home, so my mouth became my defense.

I didn't let A. D. get that far, but when he crossed the line, I would have my dukes up when he came home. There were times I would literally stand on the doorstep and dare him to come in the house, because he didn't come in at the right time. I knew he was out doing things he had no business doing. He would gamble all the rent money off, and when I would ask him, "Where's the money?" he would snap and say, "I ain't got none!" Boy that would set me off. Here I was at home waiting for him to bring his paycheck home, so we could pay bills and take care of our family, and he would come in empty handed. It not only made me angry but also gave me anxiety; I thought, "How are we going to live until his next pay?"

Somehow, we would end up friends after we fought. We would go somewhere and borrow the money for rent, and that would settle that. The next time he made a payday, we would pay back what we owed and continue doing what had to be done. We were young and immature. We had a lot to learn about each other and our lives together as a family."

But I was holding all that against myself. I wasn't allowing myself to become that new creature that the Bible speaks of. Alee told me, "Ozell, the Bible does say that you are a new creature and old things are passed away; behold all things are new."

I was raised in the COGIC where people were knocked out under the power of God all the time. But I did not know what it meant to receive Christ and develop a relationship with him. I did not know that it was the power that caused the slaying in the Spirit. When I fell out, I was indeed saved because I had repented of my sins, but I did not receive the power of God that night. That's why I had doubts about my salvation.

After Alee left, I pondered what she said about being a new creature, and I decided to return to church. When I did, God began to bless me to grow because I was serious about wanting to know God. Meanwhile, Elder Utah Smith came to our church for a revival, and at that time the Holy Ghost used him mightily! He began to preach and sing. All through-out his message, he was singing and picking the guitar. *"Ohhh, listen people, ta what I say,"* and he would pick the guitar. *"We livin' in the last 'n evil day,"* and he would pick some more. *"And my God, I know he don't lie,"* pick, pick, pick. *"Ohhh, the hand of the Lord is on this land."* He didn't sing that well, neither did he pick the guitar that well, but there was power behind what he was doing. As he preached, picked the guitar, and sang, the Spirit of God came upon me and filled me with the precious gift of the Holy Ghost, and I have not had any doubt in my heart since. I held on to the scripture Alee gave me,

Therefore, if any man be in Christ, he is a new creature: old things are passed away; Behold, all things are become new. (2 Cor. 5:17)

I knew that this was how I wanted to live because my life began to unfold before me. I was that new creature that the Bible spoke of. There was a familiar feeling that came over me. Being in the Church of God In Christ took me back to my childhood. It's something about the first ten years of my life that took root in my memories. I began to recall my grandmother in the Holiness Church and how faithful she was to her family, church, and neighbors. She was so humble and sweet. I remember how she never complained about the problems she faced daily. She was a praying woman who loved her family and God, and she proved it to us each day of her life. I remember how she would visit the sick, and she prepared warm meals for the gypsies and hobos who passed our way. They would sit in a huddle around the galley, eating and thanking Aunt Emma, all in the same breath.

But now in my life, God saved me at Looney Street Church of God in Christ, I was now experiencing what my grandmother had felt her entire life: peace and harmony in her soul. Her life exemplified how you are supposed to live as a Christian. Papa had his own makeup. He didn't let religion or nothing else stop him from living his life. If he had exemplified the Christian way of living, I probably would have been a Baptist. But I saw her life, and I will put this on any paper! My grandmother's life exemplified a Holiness life. I saw her loving people who probably thought they were her enemies. I saw her loving her neighbors as herself. She would give and do for everyone to the best of her ability. She even did for people who thought they were better than she was; she had no color line. She treated them all the same.

I saw her live a life of holiness with her husband. I've heard some say that she was afraid of Grandpa Frank. She wasn't afraid of him, He never did anything to cause her to be afraid; she was just a humble, sweet woman. I know because I lived with them. She was very loyal, and she did obey him in a childlike manner; but she knew his nature. Therefore, she did not want to do anything that would make him angry. So, she just went along with him. That's the way she had been taught—just go along with him. So, she never crossed him. She called him "F." She would tell him what she thought but she would never rare up against him, the way I did with A. D. I'm sure the Holiness Church taught her not to. I respect her to this day because she raised her children up in the way of Holiness, and then she turned around and raised her grandchildren up that same way, and that's what makes me so determined. I have asked the Lord to help me keep myself nailed down, so I can be that example that people look to when they are looking for Holiness.

Learning to Be Faithful in the Church

The pastor had confidence in my ability to get things done. He gave me a job right away. I did things I never thought I could do. After about three months of training, I began teaching the Bible band (Ironically the same auxiliary my grandmother and auntie started at Washington Chapel). This experience gave me a greater depth in understanding the Bible, because I was teaching from the Old Testament in the New in the King James Version. Somehow or another God placed me in the Old Testament. I later learned that you must understand the Old Testament to truly understand the New. Back in those days, I was doing what is considered today as cross-referencing. People would resist when they were assigned the Old Testament, but I would ask for it. I loved to teach from it. I fasted and prayed for a revelation. Some told me I would get better results if I slept with my Bible under my pillow. So that is just what I did. I don't know if it helped, but I got that word deep down in me. I will never forget the first lesson I ever taught. It was from the twelfth chapter of Romans.

> "From that scripture I told them that, at that time in the Old Testament, animals were brought to the high priest and presented before God, and they were burned, and the smoke went up as a sacrifice for the atonement of sin. In the New Testament, the Apostle Paul says to the church at Rome, "Jesus made the ultimate sacrifice and died on the cross for the sins of the world, and since you have now accepted Christ in your life, that type of

sacrificial ritual is no longer accepted." We no longer present animals; we present our bodies as living sacrifices, and the Bible tells us that it must be holy, which means to be set apart and acceptable to God, which is your reasonable service."

And the second verse of the twelfth chapter of Romans says, "*Be not conformed*," which simply means don't be molded by the world, the pattern of the world, the attitude of the world; you don't take on the things of the world, the dressing of the world, and how the world thinks, "*but be ye transformed*," which means to be made new. That's what the Apostle Paul is saying to the church: come out from the old into the new, "*by the renewing of your mind*." Everything must move with the mind. The body does not do anything the mind does not tell it to do. You see, beloved, the mind makes things transparent to the body. *That you,* not your sister, not your brother, "*might prove that which is the good and perfect will of God*." Paul went on to talk about the precious gifts that God grants us. He said,

"*For by the grace given me, I say to every one of you: Do not think of yourself more highly than you ought, but rather think of yourself with sober judgment, in accordance with the faith God has distributed to each of you*."

Because we see that sometimes when people have gifts, or because they can do something better than you, they may think they are a little bit better or live at a higher standard. So, He's saying to them, "I don't care what gifts you have, that gift was given to you to edify the church." Think about it this way, God gave this gift to me to serve the church.

Then, after I did the Bible band so well, Brother Pry (he was the Sunday school superintendent, and a good one!) wanted me to teach the primary class. Some of my first students were the White boys. Their daddy had a gas station in town, and their momma brought them to church every Sunday. I taught them for many years before I moved away from Shreveport. When I returned about ten years later for a visit, those boys had grown up and were headed to college, and they were yet in the church. They always called me, "Sister Cooper." They said, "Sister Cooper, we are yet here serving God." I was so thrilled that I did something right. Something I put in those boys made them endure even through their teen years. That encouraged me so much. I didn't quite have the full meaning of my purpose, but I do know that I was always a good teacher. I said to myself, "God must have called me to teach; if I had that kind of impact on those boys' lives, I could have that same impact on other young people also.

I knew that I must surrender all I had to Christ. The Psalmist said,

> *"Commit thy way unto the Lord; trust also in him: and he shall bring it to pass"* (37:5)

I totally committed my all to the Lord to use me for his service. I have never regretted it. Commitment doesn't mean that I commit when things are good but check out when things go bad! I realized that I must stay faithful at all costs. It came clear to me that just to be a good worker in the church was not enough. I must commit myself to the Lord.

It was when I accepted Christ that I was challenged to live out the definition of commitment in my life. My desire to commit deepened because I was more concerned with pleasing the Lord in my marriage. So, I took a more committed stand for Christ's sake. I adopted a humbler attitude, one that my husband, who was not saved at the time, could look at as an example of Christian womanhood. I knew what the Bible said in 1 Corinthians 7:13–14:

> *"And the woman who hath a husband that believeth not, and if he be pleased to dwell with her, let her not leave him, for the unbelieving husband is sanctified by the wife and the unbelieving wife is sanctified by the husband."*

There were many trials I faced in that one year from the time I got saved until God saved A. D., but I was committed to trusting Him to save my husband, and I thank God, he did. There was never a problem with my going to church before my husband got saved; he always agreed with my decision. As a baby in Christ, I did not understand my responsibility to God and my family, but I thank the Lord that my pastor at that time was a very committed man of God, and he taught me how to be a good soldier.

One day I was led to go on a three-day fast, the way I saw my grandmother do so often. A. D. was away in Houston working. Sometimes we wouldn't talk until he got back in town, so I would just ask God's protection over him. I had prayed the prayer and promised the Lord that I would serve him and commit my all to him. At that time, I gave God first place in my life. Then I became satisfied just taking care of my family. While he was away, he read a magazine article about how a young man's life had been changed even though he had done some things that he was not proud of. My husband sent me the article and wrote me a letter with one question in it: "Don't you wish that was me?" I did not even reply. He didn't know it, but I was always praying and fasting for his salvation. I did not always say it to him, but I would tell God. I was confident that it was all in God's hand, and whatever will be will be. If that was the life he wanted, fine; that was between him and God. It took all my time fasting and praying for my own life. I had to anchor myself in the Word so that he could continue to see a difference in me.

I never troubled him about getting saved. I just fasted and prayed that he would be. My pastor's wife was the one after him to get saved. One Sunday he came to church, and she asked him, "When are you going to get saved?" He promised her that the next time he came to church, he would, and he did. He was a man of his word. He was never good at telling people something that he wouldn't live up to. A. D. grew up Baptist. He grew up going to church, he knew about Christ. So, he was already familiar with the Christian life.

The next year after I got saved, I found out that my husband saw my lifestyle and wanted God to do the same for him. He had never witnessed me being humble and doing things the way I did after I got saved. When he would come in late, I didn't fight with him, I would open the door and let him in and go on back to bed. I knew that I had to treat him differently. I wasn't going to be able to fight and clown with him anymore. Eventually I lost the desire. I began to think, "He knows what he wants to do." The Spirit would just give me too fast and pray.

One year later, in that same Summer revival I was saved in the year before, A. D. and his good friends, Jack (Henry) Page, Robert, and a couple of other guys, came to church; they all sat in the back. I had been talking to Jack over the year prior. He would come over to see Christell and end up talking to me about God. He would ask me one question after another. We used to tease Jack that he was just over our house asking questions to get close to Christell. We would sit up until twelve or one o'clock in the morning, talking about God. I answered his questions to the best of my ability. A. D. didn't talk too much; he would watch my lifestyle. When the altar call came, they both went up for prayer. On the first night not much happened. Sister Clemmie, the Pastor's wife said, "Y'all come back tomorrow night and let the Lord really bless you." So, the second night only Jack and A. D. came back. And boy, they were serious when they came back the second night. I don't know who God used the most. God didn't save them on ordinary terms. They were saved to the utmost! I believe the Holy Spirit just mopped up the floor with both of them! Before the Lord saved A. D., he smoked two and sometimes three packs of cigarettes a day. When he went back home that night, he took the cigarettes out of his pocket and had the nerve to lay them up on the mantel and let them stay there until he got ready to throw them away. He didn't smoke another cigarette as long as he lived. God saved him sho'nuff. I believe he had to be saved like that so that he could be a witness to his folks. And he was.

Once my husband got saved, we became closer than ever because we had something in common. We began to have mutual friends in the church. I believe that's what drew him. We were one of the youngest couples at Looney Street, so people took us under their wings. A. D. had lots of friends, and the beautiful thing about it, when he got saved they got saved too. After I won my husband to the Lord and he became a Christian, we had wonderful parents in the Lord, Pastor B. T. Kirkpatrick and Mother Clemmie Kirkpatrick. We worked under their leadership until 1954, which is when we moved away.

Moving Towards California

Our trip to California took years. We moved across the states very slowly and deliberately. A. D. would often go before us, secure his jobs, and then send for us. Each state gave us the opportunity to move closer to the land of milk and honey, California, the state where Urie, Gloria, and Arthur said their cousins told them they could find gold on the streets.

We lived in three cities in Texas: Odessa, Amarillo, and Lubbock. The first move we made was when A. D.'s work called him to Odessa. That's where the man who owned the company lived, and the headquarters was there.

So, we moved there from Shreveport. He went first, worked a month and saved some money. We had a car but it wasn't running. A.D. put that car in the shop and got it running, and then came back for me and the kids. What we had planned to do was take the two younger children, Billy Ray and Lorell with us and leave the three older ones with A. D.'s daddy, Papa Drew because Big Momma, Missouri wanted them to stay with her. When we were ready to drive off, Arthur just went into a fit. He didn't want me to leave. He cried, "I wanna go with my momma!" I mean he screamed and cried for me, and I couldn't stand that. That boy wouldn't let me leave. And I couldn't leave my baby crying like that! A. D. said, "He will be all right." But I said, "No, he won't. He's going with me!" We had not packed any of their clothes, but I didn't care; I just boarded all of them up and left the clothes. I figured I'd buy new ones when we got to Texas.

When we got there, we had to get a house because nobody would give us a room with five kids. But what was so funny was that the lady we were renting the house from was the church mother. She rented us the house behind her house. She didn't have proper heat, and it was cold in that house! She said that the heater was good, but it burned real low. I believed she was trying to keep from burning too much gas. She and A. D. would get into it. He got so mad at her, he yelled, "Well, you come and stay in here and let me use your house if you think it's warm enough!" She responded, "You just country and wanna see your fire!" But we stayed there until we could get something better.

The company would have jobs outside of Odessa. So sometimes A.D would go off to other states to work, and finally when they had a big job in Amarillo, we moved there. That was 1954. I remember that year because my grandmother took sick; she had a stroke in the brain. So, I left to see about her. I took Billy Ray and Lorell, and the three older ones stayed back. A.D. told me, "Next time you see us, we will be in Las Vegas, New Mexico."

My concern was Momma. I had to get back to Louisiana to see about her. After being in a coma for about a week, she passed away. We took her from doctor to doctor, but anyway, she went home. I had sat up all night with Momma, and when day broke, my auntie said, "Ozell, you need some rest. Just go home." They knew she was dying, but I didn't. Before I could get home and get in the bed, they called and said that Grandmother had passed. I just couldn't get over with that. She was my momma; there are no words that can describe what she meant to me.

I waited about another week, and then we got on the train and headed toward New Mexico. We had to go all through Colorado. It was cold in that train, and when we stopped for a layover, we thought we would get some heat, but it was even colder in the train station. When we arrived in New Mexico, we found out A.D.'s company had given him a two-bedroom hotel suite—big rooms! I had a place to cook, and we all had room to rest. There was a fire that kept those hotels warm in those days. I don't know how they did it, but somehow or another, they had to fire them up, and I think the man would either get drunk or go to sleep, because sometimes we'd be burning up, and sometimes we'd be freezing out. But anyhow, we stayed there a good while, and we bought a car there, a 1952 Mercury hardtop convertible. We did have a 1946, but it started giving us so much trouble that we had to buy another one.

SURVIVING A TORNADO

One day while living in Lubbock, Texas, the kids were outside playing, and I was inside watching Television. A special report came on warning of a tornado heading our way. It was in Salty, Texas at the time. They said that it was due to arrive to our area within fifteen minutes. When I heard this, I noticed the wind started to blow. I immediately called all the kids inside. I was sitting in a chair and they all gathered around me like little chickens. And I began to pray that the Lord would keep us safe and turn the storm away from our area. This is the truth; it may have been fifteen minutes, and the updated report on the news said that the storm headed straight toward us had turned and gone in another direction. Gloria yet remembers that. She will say it today, "I heard my momma pray for us during that storm."

We lived in Lubbock, and that was the place I loved—not so much the place, but I loved the people. We lived close to the deacon and his wife. They were very friendly, and I had friends there and was in the choir at church. Being that A. D. would be away working all the time, I needed my friends. When I was just getting good and used them, A. D. said, "I believe I'll just go to California and see what's going on." His boss, the one who had done so much for him, died while we were in Odessa. The company didn't go out of business, and they told A. D., "You got work as long as you want to work for us." My husband still wanted to go to California, I think his boss's death may have had a bearing on his decision. Somehow or another, I think he was closer to the boss than he realized. He wasn't the same after the man died. He had been so nice to A. D. He brought him out there and given him a place to stay and helped him in every way possible to take care of our children.

A.D. didn't say too much, so I don't know. We didn't talk much; he worked a whole lot, so that didn't give me much time with him. When he was home, he was resting, and I was cleaning or cooking or doing something. So, when he decided to leave and go to California, it didn't bother me too much because I had friends. I'd get ready and take me and my kids to church—oh, Lord have mercy. He called me off and on throughout the month, and one day he said, "I think I'm going to send for y'all." Me and my kids and Alvernia and her kids were living there in Lubbock. Her husband, Clinton, went with A. D. to visit California. Al and I didn't stay together; we had our place, and they had their place. We lived together when we were younger, when our husbands were off working, but when we got families we lived apart.

My family along with Mother Craig
My First Years in California

I was happy to go to California and see my sister Alee, but I really didn't want to leave Texas because that was a haven for me when A. D. worked. I had friends there, I had a wonderful church home, there were plenty of young couples there at our church, so I was happy, and I did not want to leave. But I never did rebut. I never did anything that I thought would hinder A.D. from making a living. I never discouraged him. If he said do something, I just did it. If he said, "On Friday, Ozell, pack up everything. I have to be in such and such a place Monday morning," I would just start packing and putting it in the car. I think about that now, and I wonder, "Why didn't I question him?"

When he said come to California, the only thing I told him was, "When I get there, I don't want be in a small church anymore." He said, "I've already put our membership in Elder Kirkpatrick's church." That was the one time I really didn't agree. I thought, "How can he put my membership someplace, and I am not even there?" But I went along with it because we had been so blessed by this family over the years. I had been in small churches ever since I'd been saved, and I had gotten a taste of what a pleasure it could be to serve in a big church, because in Lubbock I belonged to a big church. It had lots of members and a big choir, and I was a member of the choir. I really enjoyed that choir. Bishop Carrington was our pastor. I remember he didn't believe in paying tithes, and we were taught to pay tithes; we just felt like that was our duty, so we would send our tithes back to Bishop Kirkpatrick, one hundred dollars at a time. You see, God still blessed us even though we sent our tithes back to our old church. It seemed like the more we paid tithes, the more God opened doors, because A. D. was in California a week and had a job. Alee's good friend Annie Jones told him, "I don't understand that, Brother Cooper. Some of these folks who have been here for years say they can't find a job, and you have been here a week and got a job."

Before I got to California, I'd heard it was beautiful and that there was a lot of water. I didn't want to be near water, but Alee wrote me and said she loved it. She told me, "I can sit in my backyard and see the ocean." So eventually I came around.

Me, Al, and our kids had a good time on the train traveling to California. There was a dining room where we could eat, we could sleep or talk, and we met friendly people. It was nice. Cellis and A. D. met us near Riverside. They drove separate cars because they were picking up two families. Cellis was so happy to see us. He was glad we were there. Annie Benjamin was the first person who gave us a place to stay. She gave her upstairs to us. We rented from her a short while, and then we moved in a two-story building on Thirty-First and Ocean view in San Diego.

I remember Gloria and Arthur went to Logan Elementary, and Urie went to Memorial Junior High. Things were fine at Memorial, but there was some confusion at Logan. The children were out of control, and Arthur wasn't a fighter, and neither was Gloria. They would just catch hands and run home; that's all they knew to do. A teacher told me, "This is a rugged place for your children. You may want to move further out." So finally, I told A. D., "Look like we have to sell our property back home." We held onto it because A. D.'s thinking was that we may go back. But we went ahead and sold it for $1,500, and that's how we bought our first house in California. The first house was on Hilltop, but it had septic problems, so we got our money back and moved to a small adobe stucco house on La Paz Drive. That was 1956.

When I got to San Diego, I already had five children. I had spent my life since I was just a teenager having children. But I started having babies all over.

CHAPTER 5

Commitment to Education

(1963)

Commitment to Education

Why would a woman with nine children and a wonderful husband want to further her education? This was the question a teacher asked me when I started attending San Diego City College. I felt it was something I needed to do for my children. My education was limited as a child because I had to quit school in junior high. After I got married and had children of my own, it was sad that I could not even help my elementary-school-aged children with their homework. The educational system and methods for learning had changed so drastically, that's when I felt I had to go back to school to help them advance.

The opportunity to go to school when I was a child was not as available the way it is today. When I think about my school days, it feels like a horror movie to me. I was smart enough; in fact, I was advanced two grades up. But there were many obstacles that got in my way. I had to wash, I had to clean, I had to cook, whatever had to be done at the house I did. Most of all, I had to work the fields when the harvest came due.

In an attempt to seek stability, my family moved frequently. As a result, I had to change schools often, so my education was sporadic. I shall never forget, when I was in junior high we moved near Sweet Home School. It went from primary to junior high. It was always difficult for me when I moved from one school to another because I would lose credits. I went as often as I could, but I suppose it was not enough for me to pass. When it came time for me to graduate, I went to my classroom where the grades were being passed out, and instructions were being given for those who were graduating. I was sitting in my classroom listening for my name to be called. I knew they should have called me when they got to the G's—G-R-E-E-R—but I sat there until the last name was called. One by one the children marched out with looks of accomplishment on their faces, and I was left sitting there in the classroom, alone with my heart broken. In my mind, I wondered what had happened. I was too ashamed to go up to the teacher and ask why she didn't call my name. I'll be honest, I was. I felt like she would start talking loudly, and the other children would overhear her saying, "You didn't come to school enough!" so I just got up and walked out. I cried the entire way home.

I was a smart kid. It wasn't that I couldn't learn. I just didn't have anyone behind me to push me. My dad left it up to my stepmother, and she didn't care. Because she was ignorant to the value of education, she always found something for me to do to keep me from going to school; you see, that was the problem. If she would have just let me alone, I would've got dressed and gone myself. That's the type of child I was. I was very self-sufficient. I cooked, cleaned, washed, ironed, went to school by myself, and I looked decent going too. But she would always find something for me to do. Now wasn't that the devil?

That experience was terrible for an eleven-year-old to remember. I continued to go to school, but I was so behind in my studies that I got discouraged and decided to quit and get married. That was not a solution, just a Band-Aid. It was just that at the time, I was so disappointed with my opportunities to attend school. Deep down within, I have always loved school, but I just did not get the chance to attend as much as I needed to.

After I got married, I began a family that same year, and I always knew my children needed a mother. I did not attempt to return to school until my last child was born. I would always take self-improvement classes, read books to help me raise my children, and most of all, I depended on God for what I did not know.

When I made the final decision to return to school, I asked A. D. and Gloria to help me take care of the small children. They both agreed, and I enrolled in Lincoln High, Adult Night School in 1963. Kevin was the baby. This schedule gave me time with my children at day, and they would have someone to come home to after school.

There were many snares to go through, but I had made up in my mind—I committed myself to finish what I started, and I was determined! It worked. A. D. joined me after a while, and we finished our high-school diplomas together in 1966.

My spark for learning came back, and my interest in education was piqued, so I enrolled in Mesa Junior College to begin a home nursing course. After completing the course, I received a certificate, and I went to work for Visiting Nurses of San Diego. I worked all over the city, but I was working days, and I felt like it was taking me away from my children. I was searching for a job with a more flexible schedule when a lady across the street from my house told me that they were looking for private-duty nurses in La Jolla. I joined with them and began private-duty nursing. Because nursing was in such demand at that time, I had my choice of shifts. I chose 11:00 p.m. until 7:00 a.m. The pay was good, and I was at home when my children got home from school. But A. D. had started his church in 1963, and I was obligated to many duties at church, so working Sundays became a problem. I loved nursing, but I discovered that I was away from my children too much working on holidays and weekends.

I still loved to learn, so I quit nursing and decided to go back to college and become an early childhood education teacher. I loved children, and I was amazed at the lifelong impact a preschool teacher has on the development of young children. All the material, puppets, and visual aids were overwhelming. I decided to major in child development. I knew I would enjoy teaching children, since I had taught them in my church for several years.

A friend of mine, Freda, and I had a dream to finish our degrees and start a child-development center in downtown San Diego. We had it all planned, but before we were completed, she packed our dreams in her suitcase and moved back home to New York. That crushed my plans, but I refused to quit because I was so near graduation, plus the classes were a tremendous help to me in raising my own children. I enjoyed the classes and they were interesting, so I continued until I graduated.

After completing my degree, I was offered a job as a supervisor at Lincoln High School's child-development center. There was a nursery on campus for students who had babies. They brought their children to school and interacted with them during the day. The center grew and was successful, but I did not take the position. I listened to my kids who were students at Lincoln. They did not want me to take the position, so I didn't. I regret that decision to this day.

I went to get a teaching job. They hired me at a child-development center in my neighborhood. I was close to retirement age, but I sold myself as the capable, educated individual who I was. The children loved me, the staff loved me, and the parents loved me. I gave those kids the same strict yet loving discipline that I had given to my own.

I taught at this center for several years, but I got hurt. One day I moved from my chair to catch a falling child and hurt my back. I tried to keep working, but I just could not. I began to have some serious problems with my back, and they laid me off. I was so disappointed, but I always had the attitude that "God has something better for me."

Years later, I would see adult men and women in the supermarket, and they would thank me. I did not recognize them, but they would remind me, "You were my child-development teacher, and you changed my life forever. I will always remember you, and I wish I had someone like you to teach my children." I would tell them, "Y'all telling my age now," and we would laugh. But I thank God because I have been so blessed to see how my teachings changed those children's lives.

God knows what you need and when you need it. I didn't know it, but Lorell, who was twenty-five at the time, was very sick and needed me more than when he was a child. I began to use my nursing skills to take care of him in my home. We had just put A. D.'s dad in a nursing home after caring for him five years, and Ms. Ella Mae was living with us because Mr. Joe had passed many years before, and after trying to live alone, she became blind and could no longer care for herself. While I cared for them, God allowed me to make more money than I did at my old job, and I could stay at home doing it.

As Lorell got better, I began to think about school again. I was yet committed to learning, so I enrolled in theological seminary to get my degree in Bible studies. It was not an easy road, but my husband helped me with my lesson. It was a long fight to take care of Lorell and my mother-in-law, but I did with God's help. It took me a while, but I was determined to persevere. I received my Bachelor's from Trinity Theological Seminary in Bible studies. I was seventy-two years old when I completed seminary, but I had done such extensive work in the church teaching, heading auxiliaries, and serving on the state level that I was awarded an Honorary Doctor of Divinity.

That famous question, "Why would a woman with nine children and a wonderful husband want to further her education?" has driven me to become a lifelong learner. They have told me to go home to my family, but there was a longing down inside of me for a better education. They did not know my plight, but I knew one day, it would pay off.

When the police officers would bring Billy Ray and Lorell home when they got in trouble with the law, I would tell them right in front of the police, "Y'all need to stay in school and get an education!" One day a police officer asked me, "Why every time we see you, you're talking about education? Why is it so important to you?" And I told them, "That's the only way they are going to make it in life. That's the only way they are going climb above all this negativity that they are into."

I continued to be persistent in school until I won. It was a long and tedious journey, but it was worth every minute. Thank God, my husband and daughter stood by me all the way; I owe a lot to them today.

Ozell when she graduated from San Diego City College

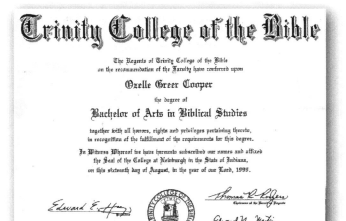

Bachelor's Degree

This is my class and my teacher's assistant. I loved them so dearly.

CHAPTER 6

Commitment through a Season of Illness

I have often wondered if my mother's illness and eventual death at my birth had anything to do with my health challenges throughout life. I have since learned that there is a clear scientific connection between the death of a mother, and future illnesses of her child. There is an entire body of research dedicated to understanding a child who is suddenly torn away from his or her mother at birth. The article "Maternal and Child Health" read as follows:

"The death of a parent early in a child's life is one of the most traumatic events a child can experience. The loss of a parent causes emotional distress and deprives the orphaned child of love, nurturing, values, information and discipline."
It goes on to say this:
"A child whose mother died at childbirth is more likely to die before the age of five, and if the life span progresses, and the child reaches adulthood, the psychological and interpersonal con-sequences of this disturbance may manifest in long-term medical and mental health problems."

But God said, "Not so!" As the psalmist said, "*I shall live and declare the works of the Lord*" (Ps. 118:17). He prepared Grandma Emma, Grandpa Frank, Papa, and eventually my sisters, Alee and MaeLee, to pick up where my mom left off. They nurtured and loved me the best they knew how.

It has always been a mystery why, to this day, I feel such a strong presence of Josie during my illnesses. Later in life that presence shifted from my mom to A. D. I prayed many nights, asking God to put those pieces together for me. Why couldn't I get her out of my mind all my life? She has been here, closer to me than some mothers on earth; I still feel her today. To some that may sound crazy, but it is the God's honest truth. I can't imagine that she just left me. Although I was just six weeks old, her death is still fresh in my mind. At times I cry just as if it happened yesterday. During my child-birthing years, I had a fear of dying. I thought I would die at the age of twenty-six or from childbirth. I was so afraid that my children would die and leave me that I slept with them on my stomach. I wanted to feel their every breath.

A PORTION OF THE MANY ILLNESSES I HAVE ENDURED.

ISSUE OF BLOOD

It was 1962, after Anita was born that I began to bleed. I flowed freely throughout the month. I flowed so long and so hard that I became anemic. It wasn't painful; it was just flowing. That's a terrible feeling, when you don't have control of your body. Dr. Ford, my doctor at the time, recommended that I have one ovary removed.

I didn't want them to take anything out of me that God gave me. I just believed that if God gave it to me, I needed it, and I would be all right with it. I was referred to Dr. Burt, and he wanted to give me a full hysterectomy. I don't believe doctors had access to the type of medical science they do today. They didn't understand the body the way they do now. The only thing they would say was, "You need have to have an operation to cure this bleeding." Medical doctors said I would just bleed to death.

I bled off and on for an entire year or more. The bleeding went beyond my normal period, and it was heavy. I believe medical science may call them fibroids today. And you know what? That's probably all it was! The first thing that came to my mind was menopause—but I was too young, I was only in my thirties. I came home crying. I told A. D. what they said, and he looked at me with a God confidence, and reassured me, "We will fast until God changes the condition." I had a lot of confidence in what my husband said because he could always back it up with the Word. God had healed me before, and I believed he would heal me again. The bleeding would not cease, so I found another doctor to get a third opinion. I believe I located him in the yellow pages. I made an appointment with him, and when he tested me, I found out that I was pregnant with Kevin. I continued to fast and pray, and God evidently shrank them, because after I delivered Kevin, I went back to the doctor, and my cycle was into its normal rhythm.

Sarcoid Disease (1972)

The real trial came in 1972 when I was sick for two years and could not take care of the children or my husband, and in turn A.D. had to learn what commitment was about. A shortness of breath caused me not to walk very far. It seemed like I was losing weight and getting weaker in my body. I had lost so much weight that I was ashamed to take my coat off; I would lie in bed and pray. When my sister Al saw how much weight I had lost, she became very concerned. She would come by and pick me up and take me to her house to cook me my favorite food, fish. She also told me to start eating Cream of Wheat for breakfast. She said that it would help to stimulate my appetite. Each day seemed to be another day for me to lie in bed, cry, and pray, hoping that some way I could get up and take care of my husband and children.

The doctor explained to me that the combination of symptoms that I had been experiencing pointed to cancer, and I needed to be admitted into the hospital for further testing. Although I was raised in a Christian home where my grandmother was Holiness, Papa was a Baptist deacon, and they both taught me about the power of prayer, I was afraid!

The Spirit took me to the thirteenth chapter of Numbers when God had promised the Israelites that they would be able to conquer the land with its indigenous Canaanite nations. Moses instructed the spies to report back on the agriculture and lay out the land. However, during their tour, the spies saw fortified cities and resident giants, which frightened them and led them to believe that the Israelites would not be able to conquer the land as God had promised. Ten of the spies decided to bring back an unbalanced report, stressing the difficulty of the task before them. Like those men who went out, I saw giants! This was what I faced once again. A suffocating shortness of breath, drastic weight loss, and the uncertainty of cancer. But like Caleb and Joshua declared, yes, giants are out there, but with God we can conquer them.

I went in for a biopsy. After some examinations the test came back, and they knew that I didn't have cancer, but I did have sarcoidosis. The doctor explained to me that with the disease, I would get weaker and weaker and my body would just dry up, because of the effect it had on my lungs. He asked me if I had smoked in my lifetime. I said no. I had never smoked. I had already lost my appetite; I had to be forced to eat. The doctor also told me how I would get where I would not be able to climb stairs, and eventually I wouldn't be able to walk to my kitchen from the bedroom.

I got so distraught until I wanted to give up. I saw this illness starting to collide with my dreams of being a good mother. All I wanted to do was take care of my family. I had faced many discouragements before and had been able to pray or read my way through it. But this time I was facing a disease that struck me down like a bolt of lightning. I did not have the physical strength to read a book, go to the water, or make recordings to lighten my dark moods. So, I had to depend on something deeper to lift my spirit. The same way I committed myself to my family, so did my husband. He would anoint me with blessed oil and pray, and Gloria tried to encourage me and keep my spirits high, but I needed something that could meet me at my bedside.

After I got out of the hospital, the doctor put me on a bunch of medicine. He gave me medicine to put me to sleep and medicine to help me move the next day. I took it all, but it seemed like none of it was working for me. I was visiting my doctor twice a week, and all he could do was give me more medicine. I had six school-aged children to take care of, and it grieved me to helplessly lie in bed and watch on the sideline as Gloria and A.D. took care of the family. A. D. would fix his own breakfast and pack his lunch and get the kids fed, dressed, and off to school. Then he would pick me up out of the bed and carry me down to the den; I was so little and so sick. He put some water and my medicine on the end table, and he tuned the radio to *the 700 Club* and put it right next to my ear. I lay there and listened to *the 700 Club* all day. I called the prayer line and told the counselor on the other end of the phone how desperately I wanted to be healed. At that very moment, she began to quote healing scriptures to me. She said, "Quote them when you wake up and quote them when you go to sleep."

A. D. and Gloria took me to and from the hospital until I finally said, "I really wish God would take me home, so I won't be a burden to my family." I said it only because it was taking their livelihood; she was busy going to school, and he was working. They both were cooking and cleaning—somebody had to do it! I didn't have enough strength to stand up in the kitchen. So yes, I did get despondent. It seemed like I would never be well again, but I began to read God's Word and think on the scripture where it is said in Psalm 107:20, *"He sent his word, and healed them, and delivered them from their destructions."*

One morning I was lying in bed before sunup, I was crying and praying for my deliverance. I thought of the twelfth chapter of Acts when Peter was arrested and put in prison, and prayer was constantly made for him by the church. The angel of the Lord stood by him, and a light shone in prison, and the angel said to him, *"Gird yourself and tie your sandals!"* and so he did. The angel then instructed him to get dressed and follow him, and he did. And Peter was freed. It was a miracle! So, I believed God would give me that same kind of miracle.

Just like with Peter, the Spirit said to me, "Get up! Get dressed and put on your shoes!" That's just exactly how He said it. He went on to say, "I want you to just go out and walk as far as you can up La Paz." Mind you, I'd never practiced walking up to this point, and I had never heard that walking was good for me. So, I got dressed and walked out, and boy was I thin. I just kind of staggered, obeying the Spirit. It's a wonderful thing to obey; there are treasures in obeying. When the Spirit of the Lord speaks to you about something, just do it! You don't know how it's coming out, but still do it. I stumbled up the street four or five houses, and then I had to turn around and come back the first day. But I felt sure that it was what the Spirit had given me to do. He said, "I want you to do that every day before the sun comes up." So that's what I did.

The second day I could go a little farther. I went to the top of La Paz to San Bernardo Terrace. And the third day…it was something about the third day. I just went on up and went around slowly to San Jacinto, and in about a week, I was coming all the way around to Olivera to Euclid and back up onto La Paz. I thought, "This is working!" I was just doing what God told me to do.

As the days went by, the dizziness lifted from my head, and I regained the feeling in my legs. I was then more determined than ever to obey the voice of the Holy Spirit. You might question this action, "How did you know it was the voice of the Holy Spirit?" I know it was because each day as I went, I felt better and could walk farther. Then we can always make our comparison to the Word of God. I thought about the ten lepers who were cleansed in the seventeenth chapter of Luke when they cried out to Jesus and said, "Master, have mercy on us!" So, Jesus saw them and said to them, "Go show yourselves to the priest," and so as they went, they were cleansed. Jesus said in the nineteenth verse, "Arise, go your way, your faith has made you well." So, I believed, and I was healed by faith. When I went back to the doctor, he said, "You don't need medicine. You are doing well." I don't even remember if I told him what I was doing; I just kept doing it.

As I kept getting stronger and stronger, I began to walk at Chollas Lake. I started with two miles, and I ended up walking sometimes five to six miles a day. Every day I felt better and better. Since I was better, A.D. and I decided to take all the kids to San Francisco to visit my cousin Bertha and her family. When we got there, I had to face a challenge that would test my courage once again. If anybody knows about the houses in San Francisco, they are made tall—three and four stories high. When we arrived at Bertha's, it was no different. I had to face those stairs. I started out and had gone to the second story, and something spoke to my heart and said, "Just climb!" and that was good for the lungs. My cousin Vanilla was down on the first floor, and I yelled down, "Vanilla, come on up here, girl!" She said, "Oh, Ozell, I can't." I knew she had sarcoidosis also, because she had come and stayed a week with us in San Diego. I said, "You can do it! Come on!" I wanted to preach to her, but I didn't. So, I went back downstairs to be with her on the first floor.

About three weeks later, they gave her surgery and she died. We had the same disease! I know this because when she came to San Diego, she was describing hers, and I was describing mine. I don't know if it's heredity or not. The doctors said maybe it had come from me living in pine thickets. I don't know. I believe when A. D. smoked, it could have affected me. You see, he wasn't cautious as people are today. He smoked in the house, the hotel—wherever he sat; he enjoyed his cigarette while he was looking at television or whatever he was doing, and I inhaled that secondhand smoke. I believe it caused me to come down with sarcoidosis. That came to me—nobody told me that—because I was nowhere near pine thickets like they said. The doctor said when he first looked at my X-ray, my lungs looked like a wasps' nest. That's the way he described my lungs to me. I told A. D., and he agreed that smoking probably did have something to do with it. We didn't know then that he should have gone outside and smoked. Later we learned that secondhand smoke was harder on the person who was breathing it than the one smoking. Eventually I regained my health. I just kept fighting, and God completely healed me. The scripture I stood on then was Matthew 10:8, when Jesus commissioned the disciples to go and heal the sick and raise the dead:

"Heal the sick, cleanse the lepers, raise the dead, cast out devils: freely ye have received, freely give."

This was a confirmation that God was not finished with me yet. He had more work for me to do. When I began writing this section, I came up with the original title, It's Never Too Late. This thought came because I overcame these illnesses and had a new life, all because God answered my prayers.

Overwhelmed (1975)

Being overwhelmed has the power to weaken already fragile emotions. It can convince you that your life is not worth living. My husband and I had been close most of our marriage, and suddenly the Lord burdened his heart with beginning a church. We started the church, and that wasn't enough. Things became so overwhelming for me. It was very strenuous, having children to take care of, cook for, shop for, educate, train, and take to their games and whatever else they were involved in. Upon all of this, A.D. decided to become a real-estate agent. He studied for the test, passed, got his license, and began practicing. This was another demanding occupation, just like the church. That was a little too much for me. It didn't seem to bother him, but I was overwhelmed! What was I to do? I was already taking care of the church, and now my husband had a career in real estate. Don't get me wrong; he was good at it! His clients would tell you that today. But it demanded most of his time. I, on the other hand, felt that I could not fight the battle any longer.

My husband was drifting away. Being a young mother, wife, church worker, holding the church together, and embracing his new career in real estate? It put me under. I wanted to get his attention, so I wrote him a letter and mailed it to him. And when he came home and looked through his mail, he saw where I had written him, and he opened the letter and sat down and read it. Normally we would sit down and talk about the situations we faced with the kids and other issues at home. But letters always got the reaction I expected from him. Neither of us wanted a divorce. I just needed relief.

I had begun to drift off into a light depression. I had been to church, got it in control, come back home, and put my children to bed—done all that I had to do. Then I'd wait for him, and he didn't come in until way over in the morning. When he did get there, I was asleep, and when he got up in the morning, he got dressed and was out the door again, because he was under pressure to show property, do all the paperwork involved in selling, and go to so many meetings. So, our communicating became almost silent, because we never found the time to talk about our need for one another. That's the kind of time real estate requires. I'm not saying all of it was real estate, but he would tell me that he was chasing clients. So yes, I did begin to kind of fall into a depression.

There is so much to say about depression that I don't want to even think about it. It can undermine your entire day. It can change your personality, and that's what it was doing for me. The doctor gave me a light dose of anti-depression medicine to help me to take to edge off. I took half of the dose of the medication for a very short while before I felt the strong need to stop. I never wanted anything to control me. I took it only because I had no one to talk to or express my desires to, and I felt like I needed immediate relief.

God has been good to me. I told the doctor my concerns about the medicine, and he suggested an alternative. He said, "When you feel yourself slipping into a depression, I would like for you to go down to Harbor Island and simply walk. Allow the water and the gentle breeze to change your mood." I wondered, "Why didn't he tell me that sooner?" We'd better be careful beloved; the medical community may not always give you the natural alternative to a physical ailment. You must be your own health advocate. But I followed his advice. He said get up early and get dressed, even if you don't have plans to go anywhere. A. D. and I adopted that as part of our ritual. We would just go down to the bay and sit and talk about how to overcome the crisis in our marriage, or even when things were good, we just went and enjoyed the scenery. It took time for the problem to be resolved, but we persisted.

Injuring My Back (1989)

I have suffered beyond measure with my lower back and spine. I was sixty-three when this injury forced me into retirement. I had a rewarding career as a teacher. It was my greatest joy to stimulate and shape young minds. I was in my mid-fifties when I landed this career. After graduating with my child-development degree, I convinced this organization to hire me, despite my age. I taught at an early childhood education center for several years, and one day, unfortunately I had an accident that caused serious injury to my back. I was in the wrong position—sitting in a chair. I lunged to catch a kid who was falling and fell to the ground along with the child. The lawyers laughed at me because they didn't think that was possible the way I did it. The injury was so serious that I couldn't even straighten up after it happened, and that's the truth! It came to my mind to back up and get against the wall. And that's exactly what I did. I sat straight with my back next to the wall and my butt on the floor. I sat there for a long time. And eventually I forced myself to get up onto my feet. When I did, I was in excruciating pain.

I went to the doctor, and he said that I had done something to the vertebrae. All up and down my legs and even to the bottom of my feet hurt me to walk. The doctor took me off the job, and for one year, I was on disability. It was so bad that I slept on the hard floor in the den because I couldn't stand to lay on a mattress. Many nights I didn't sleep at all because of the pain. I kept going to the doctor, and he eventually concluded that the only way I would ever be well again was to have surgery. But the doctor made it clear to us, "If she has surgery, it may make her better, and it may not." He wasn't even sure if I would come out from under the anesthesia. I know he had to say that because it's true! He was a specialist, and he had to give me the worst-case scenario. So, A. D. and I did what we always have done, we brought it before the family, and everybody voted no. No one wanted me to have surgery. I just went back home and kept praying for deliverance.

Eventually, after about a year, I went go back to work. But they transferred me to another site, and I worked down there until they laid me off. Some of the teachers asked me, "Ozell, what are you going to do?" I said, "If God closes this door, he got another one open, and it's going to be even better." I spoke everything into existence. I had a very positive mind, believe it or not.

They laid me off, and that same weekend Lorell's godmother came down from Los Angeles because she wanted to see Lorell; somehow or another, he wouldn't leave her mind. She was getting the feeling that something was wrong. She told me, "Sister Cooper, I'm coming to see about my child!" I didn't know it, but Lorell was deathly ill. This was on a Saturday, and I said, "Come on. We'll go check on him." I made some calls, and Lorell's girlfriend's mother told me where he was. Because I didn't run behind my grown kids—and he was good and grown! —I simply thought he was over there living with his girlfriend as usual, and they were okay.

I didn't know it, but he had been sick, got a settlement, and spent the money—on what, I don't know. All I know was he weighed eighty-five pounds! Can you imagine how I felt when I walked into that house? I almost fainted! They let him sit up there and get down that low, and the bad part about it was they didn't let me know. I got mad with them and yelled, "Why didn't y'all tell me my child was sick? At least you could have told me that!" I didn't care about the settlement that he'd gotten and spent. It wasn't the money I was worried about. I didn't say anything to her, but I said to myself, "She don't know it, but I'll be back on Monday to get my child." I couldn't do it over the weekend because, being the pastor's wife, I had responsibility at the church. I thought about it for a split second and changed my mind. Then I just told them straight, "I'll be back to get him!" That Monday I got my car, put a pillow and a quilt in there to make sure he was comfortable, and I got him in that car and brought him home.

My job thought they were being smart by laying me off, God allowed Lorell to come into the house, and I was paid to take care of him. I was blessed to be with my family and get paid. God is awesome! I mean he is awesome! They thought they were doing something big. They weren't doing anything but freeing me up to do what God wanted me to do. As I said earlier, with A. D.'s momma, and Lorell at the house, I made more money than I was making working every day at my job. And I didn't do that much, because I had children, and they would wash and dry clothes and help with Ms. Ella Mae. She wasn't helpless. At times she would let the enemy use her, but otherwise she was fine.

I thought many times about what I told them at my old job, and it was just as true as I'm sitting here today; it was better because I got to know both Ms. Ella Mae and Lorell all over again, and I was fine. I got to prepare my husband's meals, go to church, keep the house clean—whatever I wanted to do around the house. So that back injury, with all the pain and discomfort, was actually a blessing.

My life was going so well that I forgot about the lawsuit that I filed against the company responsible for my injury. The attorney called me and said, "Ozell, if you don't soon make a settlement, your case is going to expire." I asked him, "What shall I do?" He said, "Just go to court if you don't want to sue, the judge will just make a decision." So that's what I did. I didn't sue. Some people were telling me, "You can sue that company and others," but I didn't want to. My employer was the only black-owned business keeping children in our neighborhood at the time. I didn't want to have any part in destroying it. And God has blessed me tremendously as a result. If I tell you, believe me! We never wanted for anything. The attorneys said, "It won't hurt them directly," but I believed it would have. If I would have sued that child-development center, it would have affected the church that owned it and the pastor's private property as well. The attorney said, "Okay, it's your choice."

But the blessing in all of this was that God gave me an opportunity to nurse my son back to a reasonable portion of health and strength. I told them that God would give me something better! And he did. I didn't know it was going to be my child being as sick as he was, but you should have seen Lorell after I finished with him. He was just a little butterball, with his big, fat self. I laugh about that now. From 85 pounds to about 250 pounds!

PANIC ATTACKS (1980's)

It was the 1980s, and I would have panic attacks. "Ooh, child, don't say nothing!" All those years I had panic attacks, and I didn't know what they were. The doctors didn't know what to give me because they didn't know what they were. My children would ask me, "Momma why do you yell so loud when you say things?" I didn't know how to answer them then, but I now know that they were panic attacks. A. D. or Gloria would see me losing my breath, and they would get me in the car and take me to the emergency room. It seemed like I was going to smother to death. They are a mess! When we got to the hospital, all they would do was put a paper bag over my mouth and nose, tell me to take deep breaths, and send me home. But God healed me. I stand on that! I didn't even know what was wrong with me. I couldn't sleep at night, and I would say, "I know I am not crazy." I just completely surrendered my all and just told the Lord it was in his hands. I didn't think I could go any further. But I really had a rough time of it. I suffered so much.

I was up one morning about four o'clock, the way I am now, I was looking at television. This lady gave the symptoms for panic attacks, and that's when I ordered the book and tapes right there. I said, "Oh! That's what I got." I started listening to those tapes and studying the books. That was when I learned about how to manage the attacks. I learned that panic attacks stem from a sense of having a lack of control. I was feeling as if I was losing control with my family because I couldn't do for them. So out of fear, I would panic. It was the best release I'd ever gotten in my whole life; the Lord healed me through those tapes and that book. I learned how to meditate and relax my mind. I have helped many people with the tools I learned during that horrible time. I thank God for my healing.

Atrial Fibrillation (1995)

I was around seventy years old, and one day I was at my house working like I normally do. Then my heart just took off! I didn't have any control of it. I knew something was wrong, but I just didn't know what. A. D. was not at home. All I remember is I got into the car and drove to Kaiser's urgent care, because my heart wouldn't slow down. It just was gone! It beat so fast, it felt like it was going to beat out of my chest. And when they examined me, they said my heart rate was 126 beats per minute. It was out of control. They kept me there until they slowed it down. Then they suggested that I see the specialist Dr. Brown. After an examination, Dr. Brown said that the malaria I had as a child may have caused injury to my heart. So, he put me on the medication that I'm on today.

I had to continue to pray and trust God for his healing. I decided to take my mind off what the doctor can do and focus on what God is doing. Today I am yet walking and exercising.

Knee Injury (2010)

We must all press beyond our obstacles to receive God's promises. I thank God for the strength to hurdle over them. It was not easy. I have suffered with my lower back, my spine, and legs. Sometimes I could not even move my body without serious pain, so just to walk was a task. I

112

would ask my husband to stay close by to help me stand without falling, and he was always there. The knee injury was a result of the back injury that forced me into retirement.

Twenty-one years after my back injury, I fell at a twenty-four-hour fitness center as I was working out. Here we go again. Oh, my goodness! This stirred up that old injury in my back and crushed the meniscus in my knee. This time I was eighty-five years old, so the healing process was much slower. I went to Kaiser to see my doctor, and at first, she didn't take me seriously. Because I sprained my ankle on the right side and hurt the right knee, all she did was give me one crutch to help me walk, but it did not help me enough, so I went back, and she finally sent me to a specialist, Dr. Abraham, he checked my knee because of the terrific pain I was having. Well, the knee got better, but my hip, back, and legs began to hurt, and it seemed like they would not allow me to move freely. It was painful to just move my body. So, I returned to the doctor, and they shot the knee with a pain blocker, and when that didn't help, they gave me surgery to help with the pain.

I never stopped going to the fitness center. My husband encouraged me go to Joan Kroc fitness center because of the heated pool they have there. He thought it would help me, and it did. I never shall forget it, we put it on the credit card and paid it off monthly. And I went to that warm water for one year straight.

I took the swimming class two times a week and yoga three times a week, and it sure helped me to exercise that knee and keep my body moving, but it took a lot of courage because I was in so much pain.

I kept moving my body. I never stopped being faithful to church, and I even went out witnessing to people in their homes on my street. I saw a great need among my people, and I wanted to tell them about Jesus. Sometimes I could hardly lift my feet high enough to step on the curb or climb the three stairs from the auditorium to the pulpit at church, but with God's help, I made it. Those people at Antioch were there for me, two of them at a time, when I was trying to climb those steps. Now I can walk, glory to God. Thank you Lord! I prayed for the courage and energy to keep moving my body. Today I am yet fighting to win; I always say I am a winner! And I thank God for the victory. I am never defeated. I will continue to fight until God heals me completely. I know he will do it according to his word.

> *"It is his will that none of us perish but come to the knowledge of the truth. I am so much better today, and I am looking forward to a complete healing."* Amen

If I had not used these methods throughout my life, the injury that I suffered when I was eighty-five could have very well confined me to a wheelchair or in a rest home. I refused to use a walker, because it's easy to become dependent on it. I hate to say that, but you do. Sometimes now, my children see me walking with difficulty at the store and they say, "Mom, let me go and get a wheelchair." I tell them, "Oh no you don't! You can get one for you, not me." I believe you are the master of your body. I tell myself, "Ozell, you have to depend on yourself. You're going to have to get out of this car, and you are going to have to stand up using your own legs! I know your knees hurt, but, girl, you got to stand up!" When I'm home by myself, and nobody's around to catch me. I want to use my strength if I can.

Because I had a low body weight and a strong commitment to physical fitness, I recovered from that knee injury faster. My husband carried me from the room to the den. This could not have happened if I had extra weight on. But He continued to encourage me to keep trusting in God. God said, "I'll be with you always," so I said, "Lord, I'm depending on you. Help me out of this mess!" That's exactly what He did.

Exercise! All in a day's work

I said in the introduction that I want to encourage you to fight for good health, even when sickness comes your way. I also gave you my formula: Drink plenty of water, eat fresh fruits and vegetables, exercise every day, and think positive to live a full life. I am adamant about this because I have struggled with many illnesses through the years, but over time, and with God's help, I conquered them all. My body was healed from diseases that could have killed me, but God said, "Not now!"

FIVE-STAR PLAN FOR HEALTHY LIVING
1. EXERCISE
Walk. I do not mean walk when you feel like it or walk when you enjoy it, but one must devote a time of day to go for a walk. Formalize your walk. One must get as much walking in as possible. Smell the flowers, enjoy the

scenes. When I began my walking program at Chollas Lake, my eating, sleeping, and blood pressure improved. I had a heart murmur that the doctor watched, and he gave me medication for the blood pressure. Why I am writing this testimony? Because I am here to tell you that those who believe can and will be healed.

Walking is a wonderful spirit lifter, especially if we learn to walk where there is water. That's where my healing began. I walked outside in the fresh air. Soon my doctor took me off all medicine, and I was free to walk as long as I wanted to. So that is just what I did. I began to walk five miles a day and drink lots of water, and I began to regain the strength in my legs and arms. I give God all the credit for revealing to me what I needed to do for my healing.

I saw the doctor after he released me, I was in the drugstore. He called me by name and asked me how I was doing. He did not believe it was me. I told him I was fine. I told him about my walking program. Since then I have walked at minimum five days a week, one and a half hours each day. I received such good results, and I don't plan on stopping anytime soon. I love how exercise makes me feel. The benefits are amazing. I don't pretend to be a professional; I just know what it did for me, and I know I must continue to feel good and keep my weight down. My health has been restored completely. Again, When it is convenient, walk. And when it is not convenient, walk. I remember when I was in New Orleans for a women's convention, and I did not feel comfortable walking outside because I was unfamiliar with the area, so I took the stairs from floor to floor, and I quietly walked the halls early in the morning.

I would suggest that you join a group at the shopping mall or at a lake. Just take time for yourself; you deserve it. Try not to exercise at home, because it is easier to keep putting it off. But if you must exercise at home, put in a tape and get at least forty-five minutes of exercise before you begin your day. It makes all the difference. I believe my body will reap the benefits of walking for years to come. My motto is "Don't put it off. Just do it."

Sometimes I go to a twenty-four-hour fitness center and walk on the treadmill for forty minutes and ride the bike for twenty minutes. Cross-training helps to keep the body strong and firm. If I had not obeyed the

Spirit of God when he came and revealed to me to get up and walk that morning, I believe I would have died without mercy. When we refuse to obey, we run the risk of losing our blessing. Do it all with your doctor's permission.

2. EAT HEALTHY

I began to follow the rules about five fruits and vegetables. Most of the time, I eat three vegetables (Broccoli, green beans, carrots, mixed vegetables, collard greens, cabbage greens, turnips, and spinach); and two fruits (Peaches, nectarines, apples, oranges, pears, grapes, and melons of all kinds.) Eating fresh fruits and vegetables is the best because you will benefit from the fiber. I also began to eat whole-grain cereals (Oatmeal and Cream of Wheat, whole-wheat bread, and whole-grain rice and pasta), as well as corn bread, corn, potatoes, and all kinds of beans—pinto, red beans, and black-eyed peas. These foods, if eaten in moderation, will have an amazing impact on turning your health around. I began to eat lean, broiled chicken, turkey, and fish to help keep my blood pressure down. It was amazing how much better I felt when I began to eat healthy.

3. LOSE WEIGHT

You can eat a wide variety of food you enjoy and yet lose weight. You must eat enough to keep the body metabolizing; you cannot starve yourself. I have learned healthier ways to cook my own food at home. I stay out of fast-food restaurants. Limit your salt intake. You will become reacquainted with your taste buds. The flavor will surprise you.

I keep my weight in control by eating the right food and making sure I don't overeat. That's what takes away your health, overeating. That's the truth! It just doesn't take much food to carry your body. So, if you can make it up in your mind to go that direction, it would be better for you in the long run. In my younger life, after age forty, I learned a lot about food and how to handle it. How to let food be something I need, not just desire. When I was in my nursing course, we learned so much on how to eat to be healthy and how important it was not to get caught up in a cycle of eating and putting on weight and then eating because you became discouraged that you had put on the weight. I was grateful to learn these principles and bring them home for my family.

4. Drink Water
Drink at least eight glasses of water a day. Start early in the morning, and that will make it much easier to get all your water in. Interestingly, the more you drink, the easier it is to drink. You feel energized. Water will give you a refreshed feeling of being alive. I cannot express how much our bodies need water. When I learned it, I began to carry a water bottle. At that time, it was not popular to do so. Of course, that was in the seventies, and this way of life was not popular then. But now I notice just about every speaker at church and people who exercise carry a water bottle. Sometimes it is not hunger that's bothering you; it is the lack of water, in my opinion. Water can help with weight problems if used correctly. Drink water before you sit down to eat your meal, and it will help you limit your food intake. I am a witness that there are miracles in drinking water.

5. Rest
The body as well as the mind can be relaxed after a good workout. This is just as important as eating healthy and drinking water. The body needs six to eight hours of sleep each night. Exercise helped me with this. Each time I work out, I am rewarded with a good night's sleep. Before I began my walking program, I was sleep deprived. Some nights I would not sleep at all. At one point I was hospitalized for an illness for seven days, and I did not sleep one wink. So, I know what it means to lie awake all night with no sleep at all. But when I began to exercise, that all changed for me. I began to sleep from six to eight hours a night, without medication.

When I began to learn how to take care of myself, to put myself first, I took what I learned about taking the proper rest and applied it to my life.

I take a nap every day. I don't just lie across the bed or in a chair. I take off my day clothes, and I put on soft pajamas, just like I would at night. I get in the bed under the cover and turn off the lights, the TV, and any other device. I shut the blinds and go to sleep. When you do this, you won't be jumping up for everything. Thirty minutes to an hour of this type of rest is a marvelous way to begin the second half of your day.

Some may ask, "Don't you get tired?" Yes, I get very tired, but I know how my body feels when I apply these disciplines. And, I allow the memory of how I feel when I do apply them to drive my decision to continue to do it. I tell my kids, "everything I don't want to do, that's exactly what I do." I call this my five-star health plan: exercise, eat healthy, lose weight, drink water, and rest. You will never regret it.

CHAPTER 7

Conclusion of Commitment Through A Season of Illness

Grandma Emma's Faith Carrying Me through My Illnesses

You know what? I was such a strange kid, and it followed me into adulthood. I just believed that God could do anything. I believed whatever was wrong with me, God could make it right. I don't know, Grandmother put that in me. It seems like even today my grandmother will come back into my spirit and support me in my prayers! I absolutely believe that there's nothing too hard for God if you would just trust him and give it all to him. Some may ask, "What do you mean by that?" I would answer, "Give him your all and ask him to use it for his glory, whatever it is!" And my grandmother was just that way. I can hear her now saying, "All God can't do, let it go undone!" She just put her life into it.

The law put her under a "peace bond" for her faith. Someone that she took care of died, and she was accused of allowing it. Don't you know that people are going to die anyway? When people took sick, their family would bring them to Momma for healing. She was already a midwife, so people trusted her. She would care for strangers the same way she did for her family. She would take that polace cloth, and lay it on our heads for the fever, then she would go to praying! We didn't go to the doctor, and no doctor came to us. But guess what? We were healed. And many people were healed under her care. She would cook some greens, the baby ones. I should explain. After those mustard greens were planted, and they began to come up, they were little and tender. It was tradition that when you were sick, they would pull those little tender mustards up by the root, cut the root off, wash them, and cook them just enough to get a strong liquor, which was the juice. They would give you that liquor, and over time your appetite would increase, and that's when the healing would begin.

Grandpa Frank mixed special medicines from the root of plants in the woods. But I don't know if she used those mixtures on the people she cared for. I wouldn't dare say that, because Grandmother didn't believe in nothing but her blessed oil, prayer, and food that came from the ground. And by her doing that, God would do the healing. I know because He did it for us!

The law said the next time somebody took sick and came to her for healing, if she did not turn them over to the doctor, she was going to prison! That's the way it was. Her prayer, anointed oil, and home remedies made her responsible for those people's death. I don't know who told the law, but somehow it got in the wind. This meant she had to stay away from healing sick people. According to the law, her methods of diagnosing and treatment weren't successful. The way I figure, it wasn't her methods; it was God that she trusted.

My grandmother meant everything to me; I mean everything! When I hear people describe her as docile, I get indignant. They say that because she never rebutted my grandfather. I will say this again, and I will take this statement to my grave, yes, Frank Washington was strict, but you know what? My grandmother was saved, and at that time they taught you to hold your peace. They taught you to be quiet; they taught you that saved wives were not to rare up and fight back. I believe that's the way she was. She never told me, but I believe that's what she was doing. And she was loved by everybody. It is possible that even those people who sentenced her to the peace bond loved her. I believe the law may have done that to protect her. So rather than putting the responsibility of folks' death on her, the law wanted her to call them, so they could take over the responsibility. I think that's the way it was. Or maybe that's just how I fixed it up in my mind.

It may sound unreasonable to you, but what I saw her do has brought me this far all these years. I told them at my church, Antioch, "Until you lay me out here, or wherever you lay me, I am going to hold on to God's unchanging hand because God has brought me this far. It is His Word that has carried me through all these years."

I think about when I was raising my children, and my, my, my, I want to cry sometimes. My kids didn't know how sick I was all those years. They didn't know all the illness I had overcome. I would be in bed for weeks

124

at a time because I couldn't stand up; I was too weak. I was a young woman. I would be ashamed because I thought, "I need to be doing for my children." That was always on my heart. I attempted to keep it from my kids because I didn't want to worry them, but I should have sat them down and told them what was going on with me. Anita and Kevin were too young to remember. Delphine may have noticed but she never said anything about it, but Steve somehow discovered it. He would stick his head into my room and tell me, "Momma, I got to go. My friends are waiting on me," and while he was in there, he would look into my drawers and see all that medicine. He says now, "I remember my mother having a drawer full of medicine," and I tell him, "Son, I had lots of medicine, but it wasn't a drawer full."

Many people didn't expect me to live through that, but I say that A. D. and Gloria fought for me! When I was sick, I would slip and say, "Y'all let me die." Now how did I think my small kids would survive if I died? That goes to show you how I wasn't thinking straight. I now think about how my illness affected my children. I know it affected Gloria. She never told me how she felt. She would just cry. She felt so bad for me.

These seasons of illness have proven to be seasons of miracles and triumph. God's goodness and mercy has covered me down through the years. I hurdled over two autoimmune diseases, knee surgery, a back injury, a breast lump, uncontrollable bleeding, malaria, overwhelming depression, anxiety and panic attacks, atrial fibrillation, pneumonia, and more. The doctors predicted that before I turned seventy, I would have plastic heart valves and would be in a wheelchair because of the crippling arthritis I had as a child.

It was through all of this that I learned to trust in God's unchanging hand. I prayed for God to drastically change my condition. Some people may pray only once for what they are petitioning from God. I, on the other hand, constantly seek God's face. I reminded him what the scriptures say. I remind him how he has made a way and healed my body before. It is this type of prayer that has taken me through horrific pain.

Jesus Works

I quote my healing scriptures until I go off to sleep. And, as I wake up through the night I continue to quote them. When I can't think of them, I just say, "Jesus," and I tell you that room is sanctified because I have quoted my scriptures and read my Bible, and I find out that it works, Jesus works! Saying his name works because the Bible says,

> *"Neither is there salvation in any other: for there is none other name under heaven given among men, whereby we must be saved"* (Acts 4:12).

Beyond the healing, I prayed and asked God, "What would you have me to do?" I knew God had a reason for my being ill, so I sought the answer. After praying, it was revealed to me how I had been so faithful working in the church, but now the Holy Spirit was revealing to me, "relationship." The Spirit showed me that I needed a closer relationship with Jesus Christ. God was saying, "Going to church is fine; everyone needs to go to church. But now the Holy Spirit wants a closer relationship with you." I had been in the church for many years, and I had been faithful, studied the Bible, taught Sunday school class, taught Bible band, and served as coordinator of women in the church. I taught in seminars, but I needed to build a relationship with Christ. First, I needed to open a line of communication between me and Jesus Christ. How would I do that? I thought the very best way was to pray until I got the answer. Then I needed to meditate and allow the Word of God to answer me back. Finally, I needed to discipline myself to make God's Word my life's foundation.

This is the main purpose for writing this book in the first place, because I must tell the world that God answers prayers! I believe I need to share this healing and many other things with those who may not know Christ and the departing of their sins and being filled with the Holy Spirit. It is such a blessing to live to tell the story.

CHAPTER 8

Commitment To My Boys, Billy Ray and Lorell

(1965-1986)

It is natural for people to think differently when they enter school; I was no different. School exposed me to professional opinions and academic theories, while A. D. was concerned with other things, such as work and providing for his family. This type of exposure can be dangerous. It can even cause a breakup, because how can two walk together unless they agree?

I have always felt like I owed my children as much exposure as possible. A. D. and I were very young when our first three children were born, and I believe God had a lot to do with their training; because we really didn't know what we were doing. And, did not understand what it took to raise children. I give God the credit.

For some reason I was not satisfied with that. From where I stood, it seemed as if the first three fell in line only to please us. That was good! They were great children. They were full of respect, they loved and reverenced God, and they did well in school, but I wanted more.

So, with Billy Ray and Lorell, I began to seek out a different structure for their lives. When I went back to school to get my high-school diploma, I was impressed with this book I had read about, *How to Raise Children*, by an expert in the child-development field. It was at that time that I decided to use some of his suggested parenting techniques with my two boys. A. D. strongly disagreed, but I was dead set on using some of this doctor's methods to assist me in raising Billy Ray and Lorell.

I allowed Ozell and my educated opinion to creep in, and then God just moved out of the way. I started thinking I would read secular books and get some of my answers. I wanted my children to be professionals, and I thought that if I raised them by professional advice, they would receive all that they needed to compete in a professional world. I said to myself, "If these methods worked for other parents, they would also work for me."

One of the doctor's suggestions was to allow children to move from one stage of development into the next without any pressure or suggestions. He said that they would develop more fully if you allow them to work their way out of situations, rather than force them to do things your way.

So, while they were very young, I began to allow Billy Ray and Lorell to speak and act with more freedom than I had with my other children. I did this because I felt that they would know how to stop when they were ready. I remember a time when I was in the waiting room at the doctor's office, and I allowed them to go from the Colored section over into the White section. I didn't stop them like I would have the older kids. I tested those methods. If they didn't feel afraid or apprehensive about going, I wasn't going to impose apprehension on them and make them afraid. I let them have an opinion and express it without fear of retaliation. I believed it would translate into high self-esteem. I didn't want them to live under a guilty cloud.

Although I knew God and trusted him for my life, I put these two boys' futures in my own hands. I did what I wanted to do instead of completely trusting God's Word. I didn't seek his will for Billy Ray and Lorell's lives the same way I had done for my first three children. I gave my thinking over to the book, and I did not let God's way be my only method. God gave me my desire but brought leanness to my soul. It wasn't that I didn't love or trust God. I just thought somewhere in my heart and mind that I just wanted to go to another level.

As with all my children, I saw greatness in those boys. Lorell was smart and talented, and Billy was quick to master things. Arriving on this earth less than two years apart, they were very close. It was as if they were connected soon after birth. What one liked, the other one liked. I began to teach them how to defend themselves and how to love, respect, and take up for one another. They quickly caught the mantle and began to operate like one person; Billy was just a copycat. I remember them so vividly in elementary school. If Lorell didn't like something in school, then he would convince Billy not to like that same thing. If they got in trouble, they never denied it, but their full-time jobs were to convince me that it was somebody else's fault: the teacher or other kids. Not theirs!

When they were about six and seven years old, they were walking home from Knox Elementary School and decided to throw a rock at a city truck. Little did they know; the city worker saw them. The rock hit the windshield and cracked it. They got scared and tried to run, but the man came from out of nowhere. He caught them and demanded to know where they lived. They declared to that man that they lived at 1040 South Forty-Fifth Street. That's where their grandmother and grandfather lived.

So, he got them in the truck and took them there. Ms. Ella Mae answered the door, and the city worker explained to her what happened. She immediately called me and said, "Ozell, this man got your two boys, and he wants your address." I told her, "Put him on the phone!" I gave the man my address and told him to bring them home.

When they arrived, he sat down and explained the situation. Once he left, I asked Billy and Lorell did they, do it? They both said yes, and that they were sorry. I didn't whip them, nor did I punish them at that time; I probably should have. But the reason I didn't was because, as a mother, I did not want them to get so afraid of punishment that they would resort to going outside the home, the way they had just done with their grand-mother. I didn't want them to fear coming home to their parents and tell us the truth. I told them, "I'm not going to whip your behind because I don't care how bad the situation is, I don't want you be afraid to come to me for anything!"

I enrolled them both in Cub Scouts, and I was even the den mother. I tried to meet their social and educational needs. I saw that it wasn't enough, so they started little league. Lorell excelled in sports, up to the point that when he was at O'Farrell Junior High, they wanted to put him in the Junior Olympics. But during one of his sports physicals, they found out that he had a heart murmur, so he had to stop sports altogether. I believe this discouraged him from going to school. From that point on, he would say that he was going to school but went over to his friend's house and drank beer, and Billy followed.

OUT OF CONTROL

My boys were smart, and they could have excelled if they had stayed focused. But when they were barely teenagers, they began to defy all social boundaries. They began to run away from home. I stopped and asked God to help me, like I did with the first ones, but it wasn't as effective because they were disobedient. I felt as if I ruined their lives by thinking they would come out of it. Their dad and I would go find them and bring them back, but they would not stay. They would just leave over and over again.

When they were fourteen and fifteen, they decided to get married. We were happy because we knew the two young ladies whom they were marrying. We thought that it would help them settle down and take responsibility. But there was a house down the street on the other side of La Paz that seemed to constantly draw them.

They were young, married, and on their own. They could do whatever they wanted to, and that's what they did. They were in and out of the California Youth Authority for petty crimes. Later, they began breaking the law, but now they were going to prison. Their behavior almost destroyed me and my family. The other children were disturbed because of their conduct.

At that time, I felt like there was no way of reaching back. The damage was done. With perfect hindsight, I watched what I thought were my teaching, play out in their lives. Drug overdoses, alcohol, gangs, and prison were slowly taking them under. I couldn't stand to see Billy laid up in a hospital bed, just a kid, in a coma. For four days he was dead to the world! Lord, have mercy. We cried out to God right there in that hospital. We still had younger children to care for. Kevin, Anita, Delphine, and Steve sat in the waiting room way over into the night while we prayed the

Spirit of death away from our son. The ambulance had picked him up out of our yard after his so-called friends dumped him there. They left him to die. My next-door neighbor Earlene, bless her heart, called me and said, "Mrs. Cooper, Billy is outside on the grass, and I don't know if he's all right." She called the ambulance, and sure enough, he was in coma. We stayed out at the hospital the entire time. And, on that fourth day, he woke up and asked for McDonald's. Oh, glory to God! Don't tell me what God can't do.

Their situation became seemingly impossible for me to deal with. I felt so discouraged and disappointed with my parenting. I felt like I had failed Billy and Lorell. It was a time of turmoil for me. The problem became so stressful that it threatened my relationship with A. D., but we remained strong and committed to one another. I would talk, and he would listen. He would encourage me to not give up. He never once said, "I told you so!"

Many days I was afraid that I was not going to ever see my boys come back home again, but I kept on praying. People prophesied on my boys; they said all of what was going to happen, that they were being turned over to a reprobate mind. I don't listen to what people say about my kids. Sometimes they got kids worse than yours, and they are out trying to tell you about how bad yours are. I began to cry out to God for a change.

I stayed on my knees for fourteen years, praying and fasting before God for my boys. I had others pray for them. I was so desperate for God to change these boys. I wrote a radio evangelist and asked him to pray for them to change. He wrote me back and said, "Those boys must have the desire to change on their own." I knew this in my mind, but the Holy Spirit spoke to my heart and said, "God can change the mind." I never gave up hope for them to be saved. I always knew God was going to save them. Nothing anyone said to me about them discouraged me. I just continued to desperately cry out to God on their behalf.

Out of all that was happening, I wanted them to stay at home. I wanted them close to me. I figured that they would be safe at home; whether they were high or not, I could watch over them. But when their dad blurted out the emphatic "No! They have to go," my heart sank. In fact, a piece of it tore each time they left.

I was so sick that I began to bleed. I had panic attacks, and the doctors thought I had cancer. They put me in the hospital and gave me a biopsy. I was lying up there, sick enough to die, because we couldn't find our boys. They had been gone a long time. A. D. would search and then come back and tell me that he couldn't find them, and I would cry and send him back out there. I figured they had to be somewhere, hopefully not somewhere dead.

Finally, A. D. found them and brought them up to the hospital. And when they walked in, they were both dressed up in new clothes, smiling and laughing like they had just seen me the day before. I decided that day that I was done worrying about them. If A. D. wanted them to go, then they would just have to go. I still had my younger kids to raise, so that's what I was going to do. I was going to live my life. I felt that I had to trust my husband because, after all, it was my fault that Billy Ray and Lorell were in this condition; at least that's what the enemy wanted me to think! But not so. Through it all, God had me in his arm of protection.

I had to learn that one person cannot be committed and the other not. Both must say the same thing. And I'd begun to learn to trust that their father was in control as a father. Finally, one night in a dream, I saw my two boys walking down our street, La Paz Drive, with Bibles in their hands, working for the Lord and witnessing for Jesus Christ. I want you to know at that time, they were yet out doing their thing, but I got satisfied about them.

Kevin came home and said, "Mom, people are saying my brothers are going to die in the streets." I said to him, "No, they will not die in the street. God is going to save them and bring them home." It was not long until their dad said, "The boys want to come home to stay for good." I didn't know if this was God's timing for them to come home, because they had come and gone so many times before. But, I saw how serious he was, so I agreed to have them come home. Yes, they were ready to stay home and live for God. I knew they were sick, but I didn't know they were as sick as they were. The doctor told me that Billy had checked himself out of the hospital, while his blood pressure was up to "stroke" level. That any minute, he could die from a massive stroke. And I had picked Lorell up out of the streets because he couldn't walk. He would just fall right there in the streets and couldn't get up. People had to come and get me from the house to go down to Paul Lowe's store and carry him home. As parents, we were both at a loss for what to do next? Billy was suffering from kidney disease, and Lorell had a mysterious form of multiple sclerosis.

My Boys' Sickness

For a mother, seeing the decline of her child's health is devastating. Watching my sons deteriorate was more than I could mentally, emotionally, physically, and spiritually bear. When they became ill, they retreated to my little babies. I had overwhelming feelings of hopelessness, fear, and anxiety. I prayed, and God told me how to begin to teach them—not so much for their healing, but I prayed for God to save their souls. That was more important to me than healing.

Billy told me that the Spirit of God spoke to him on my back porch. It said, "You've tried everything else…try me!" Billy answered the call with the scripture from Isaiah 8:6:

"Then I heard the voice of the Lord saying, 'Whom shall I send? And who will go for us?' And I said, 'Here am I. Send me!'"

This was a beacon of light and hope for Billy.

The spirit moved on my entire house. Those very boys whom I birthed into this world were on fire! I sat them down at my dining room table, and I not only led them to Christ but also gave them a charge to get busy doing God's work winning souls. I instructed them to become a part of something bigger, to take their leadership role in society. And that's just what they did!

We began to have devotion every day. I said to them, "You both need to do more than just go to the church for prayer and service each week. You need something to keep you busy while helping others." Then God began to move upon Billy's heart to start a ministry.

Wings of Freedom

The organization was born at my dining table. One-day Billy said to me the Holy Spirit had burdened him to help men and women who needed help with their children while their mates were in prison. The name God gave him was "Wings of Freedom," which came from the Bible. Billy began to work by getting federal grants. The organization began to grow so much that he had to get a place to expand. The City of San Diego gave them a building on Thirty-Second and Market to set up their offices. These boys would go out and clean vacant lots and paint. As they found work, the Lord blessed this organization, and it grew. Billy put on parades for the city where the mayor walked alongside of him in the name of peace. God blessed his work, and many people were saved.

The mayor appointed him to the gang task force, and Billy organized the first ever gang truce in San Diego. He fought to change the names of schools, and he took the message to the streets that Jesus could save them too. He went to prisons and preached the gospel. He went to churches in the city and preached to help young people to know that they needed to change. He preached a changed gospel.

He told his testimony of how God had saved him from prison and sickness and death. God saved many people because of his testimony. Today we have people who are yet serving in Antioch who were saved and came to the Lord through his ministry. Billy was facing a forty-five-year prison sentence. Although he had given his life to God, his past doings caught up with him. The authorities had built a case over the course of several years, and they finally had enough to put him away for the rest of his life. Glory to God, we got busy praying! But we got even busier working to eradicate that entire situation. We called in judges and lawyers, bishops, and community leaders to be a powerful force that would change this situation around. With God's help we prevailed, and that sentence was overturned, right there in the Chula Vista Criminal courthouse in Chula Vista, California.

Billy Ray and Lorell strayed from their training. They both became prodigal sons like in Luke 15:11–32. This son asked for his portion of his inheritance, and his father gave it to him, and the son went out and wasted it on frivolous living. But one good part was he came to himself, and so did my two young men. They came to themselves, and they came home. Over the next seven years they dedicated themselves to service in the Army of the Lord. They worked, even when the doctor told Lorell that the form of multiple sclerosis that he suffered with was crippling; like a wild vine in the rainforest, it had choked out nearly every nerve in his body, leaving him confined to a wheelchair.

They worked! Even when the bones in Billy's feet were crumbling under his fragile body. He would hop from one foot to the other while he stood and had conversations because the pain was so bad. He sat in dialysis for several hours every other day because his kidneys were 100 percent diminished. They worked! When the doctor told Billy that his twenty-eight-year-old body was equivalent to that of a seventy-two-year-old man, and that he had high blood pressure and congestive heart failure. The outcome did not look good in man's eyes, but God had the final say.

I cried out, "God, don't let my boys die in the streets." I had prayed, and I honestly believe he heard my cry. Both Billy Ray and Lorell died, but not on the streets! They were busy working for God until He said, "Enough!"

Billy was a great witness for God in the streets and became an ordained minister, and Lorell became a deacon. They worked with passion. I am telling you this story to let you know that I serve a God of second chances. You my friend, have a great opportunity to go to school and give yourself the gift of an education, to go to college and find the missing part of your life. Make good of your second chance.

The Death of Our Boys

This was the most challenging thing that has ever threatened our marriage. Billy was in intensive care. He was dying, and I could not stand to see him pass away. They asked him if there were any final words he wanted to say to me. He looked in my eyes with a yes, but said no. I walked towards the door, and I had not made it to the other side when they said, "He's gone." A couple of months later, I went to Anita's house in Los Angeles to get some rest, and A. D. called me and said that he walked into Lorell's room that morning and he was dead, just five months after we buried Billy.

Billy's death forced me to the edge of endurance, but then Lorell's death pushed me beyond what I thought any human being could bear. It sapped all the life out of me. And that put a strain on the entire family. No one can know what it is like unless they have gone through the same thing. I grieved for two years. My mood sank to an all-time low.

I cried and thought, "I would be better off if God would take me home." Even though I had seven children left to love and cherish, Gloria had to remind me, "Mother, you still have children here who need you." Oh! My heart breaks at the very thought of them both, dead. The question I kept asking myself and God was, "Did I cause this tragedy? Did I teach them right about life? Or did I keep them too close, so they felt deprived of life?" Originally, we thought the tug-of-war between our traditional, spiritual child-rearing techniques, that doctor's methods, and the streets were the cause of this collision. I thought about all those boys out there destroying their lives, and my boys were doing well. "Why are they here and mine are gone?"

The guilt I suffered after they were gone was consuming. In my own limited thinking, I wanted to go to sleep and never wake up; I just could not imagine life without them. Yes, we had difficulties we had to overcome as a family, but did it have to come to this?

I was overwhelmed with emotions, and more came to mind. Through all of this, it was difficult for A. D. and me to keep our relationship alive. This situation invaded our marriage and stripped us of all that we had to give.

Over time, God's Word delivered me from all the guilty stain. So, if you don't understand anything else I wrote, be sure to allow God's Word to guide you in your child-rearing. Don't forsake the Word of the Lord. Keep God's Word in your heart, and plant it in your child's heart. Proverbs 22:6 says,

"Train up a child in the way he should go and when he his old, he will not depart from it." The reference verse 2 Timothy 2:15 says, *"Study to show thyself approved unto God, a workman that needeth not to be ashamed, rightly dividing the word of truth."*

LESSONS I LEARNED DURING THIS SEASON

This season taught me that I must trust and lean on God. Keeping a relationship together when a tragedy like death strikes a family can be very stressful. It can make you forget you even have a spouse. But having communication and a commitment to never give up, and keep moving toward your goal, can work wonders for the two of you. It's not just the marriage; it is the relationships of every individual in the family. There must be an undying trust and love between them because there are missing links. Billy and Lorell became those missing links.

All is well with my soul because God knew our hearts. We were babies having babies. We carried out our parenting roles with honor and pride, and we promised God that we would build a nation that would change the world; that we would teach our children about love and grace, and we would teach them to reverence God and respect nature. We loved them with strict discipline, in hopes that all would be well.

I thought A. D. was too strict on his children, and he always said it was me and my ideas about the doctor's book that contributed to this tragedy. I didn't argue, I just took the criticism, asked God to forgive me and went on. Because I thought at one time, it was me. But now I don't believe it. Because I didn't teach them anything contrary to what I taught my first three children. I only added to it.

For years I lived with the guilty stain, but I can't say enough how God and his Word have taken that away, and now I have found such comfort in the Word. Many have asked me, "How does the Word do that? How can you be relieved by the Word of God?" Over time, I would have emotions that I could not identify. When I read the Word, it would give me a deep-seated peace down in my spirit. My broken heart began to mend, piece by piece. There were so many people who would interfere with Billy Ray and Lorell. There were people we knew personally—people at the church—who would hide them out, let them smoke, and do drugs when they knew it went against our principles.

Isaiah 54:4 reads,

> *"Fear not, for you will not be ashamed; be not confounded, for you will not be disgraced; for you will forget the shame of your youth, and the reproach of your widowhood you will remember no more."*

It also says in John 3:17,

> *"For God did not send his Son into the world to condemn the world, but in order that the world might be saved through him."*

And finally, Psalm 103:8–12 reads,

> *"The Lord is merciful and gracious, slow to anger and abounding in steadfast love. He will not always chide, nor will he keep his*

anger forever. He does not deal with us according to our sins, nor repay us according to our iniquities. For as high as the heavens are above the earth, so great is his steadfast love toward those who fear him; as far as the East is from the West, so far does he remove our transgressions from us."

There are many more scriptures that I don't have time to quote. I was so desperate for spiritual healing that I would write them down on flash cards and read them to myself every day. I put them on tape and listened to them in my car; I got them down in my spirit.

BROKEN-HEART MENDING

There were times when A.D. and I tossed the blame back and forth like a hot potato. We questioned ourselves, 'What did we do differently?' We finally reached the conclusion that it was not only us, it was the environment that we had little control over.

Black American culture underwent a paradigm shift in the late sixties and early seventies. History took a defining turn. The world as we knew it had changed. Thinking back, it may have been difficult for many parents during this time of free love, sex, drugs, and Black panthers. Other races should look at the example that has been made of Black America, and the shifts that can come into a community and make a damaging impact without notice. I should have stopped and asked God to help me, like I did with the first ones, but I didn't. I tortured myself year after year by thinking, "All I did was ruin their lives by thinking they would come out of it." Thank God, he was with me through it all. I may not have put him first, but he never left me. To God be the Glory!

The Holy Spirit assured me that integrating the doctor's methods did not cause all that destruction. Yes, the book did pull me away from some of our traditional methods; those time-tested, tried-and-true teachings of the Bible. But I only had the best intentions for those boys, and I know for sure that I was not completely to blame for the way they turned out. It was also that grandmother on the other side of La Paz who would hide them in her house and say they weren't there and allow them to have drugs in her house. I never saw it, but I honestly believe they did. We would be looking for them after they ran away when they didn't want to obey. We knew those boys had run to that house, but those people would say that they weren't there. They could always take refuge in that house. Before it was all over, Billy said there was a demon in there. Before he died he said, "I want some men to go with me over there and pray." Thank God there was a good end, for me and for my boys.

When I later learned that all six of my boys had gone astray from our core teachings in one way or another, I was relieved. With all our boys, we had similar methods of child-rearing. I then had to ask the question, "Am I giving this doctor too much credit?" If it was the case that this book was the reason, then the other boys should have been perfect, and they weren't.

We accepted our failure, and A. D. would even preach about how God's children failed. Because people in the church and the community will remind you of your failure, they will persecute you and taunt you because you are living examples. At Billy's funeral they said that he did more in seven years than some bishops. The altar call was just full of young people giving their lives to Christ. It is because of their lives, that the course of Antioch and Southeast San Diego are changed forever. Lives were changed, and doors opened because of this testimony. To this day people in this area know and remember them both, and the work they did to change the community.

Billy and Lorell died too young. They were too vigorous and full of life, and they were far too precious to all of us to disappear so quickly from our lives. I pray that you can see the importance of sharing, planting, and giving the Word of God first place in your child's life.

There is a great responsibility that comes with transparency. Me being transparent in this memoir was difficult, but it has set my soul free. I pray that it will do the same for those reading it. As I wrote in my journal, I was straightening it out in own my mind. And now I am releasing it to shed a true light on my journey.

Moving Forward

After two years of crying under a dark cloud, my broken heart began to heal. One Sunday I was sitting up in church, and the Lord spoke to me (you know the Lord speaks to me just like another person, just like a daddy). He said, "Get up! Stop your crying." I was sitting up in Antioch, and after two years, I was still crying. He said, "You've cried enough." Then the 119th Psalm came to me:

> "Blessed are the undefiled in the way, who walk in the law of the Lord...They also do no iniquity: they walk in his ways...Then shall I not be ashamed, when I have respect unto all thy commandments. I will praise thee with uprightness of heart, when I shall have learned thy righteous judgments...I will meditate in thy precepts and have respect unto thy ways. I will delight myself in thy statutes: I will not forget thy word."

It's a beautiful scripture, and to this day, it blesses my heart every time I read it. God helped me to realize that the sun shines just as bright today as it did in the days prior to Billy Ray's and Lorell's deaths. I even had a vision of Billy leading a host of young people, and Lorell came to me as an angel. It was then that I thought, "Here I am wasting away from missing you, and you are up in glory praising God!" I got myself up and started living. God helped me to realize that they made their own choices to live the life they did, and they died because of their choices.

I wrote this story to show the evolution of my parenting styles and their effects. And I also wrote it to encourage young parents to explore alternate child-rearing methods but stay on the same page when doing it. A couple must not be divided, because children know when you are. I am not saying that books, tapes, and seminars don't help. I believe parents should solicit all the help possible when raising their children. But please take my advice: always include God's way and his Word when raising your children. You must come to an agreement with one another and then apply it to the children. It is not always easy to agree because each person is an individual, with his or her own mind, will, and emotions.

CHAPTER 9

Learning Balance with my Last Four Children

(1960's - 1970's)

A well-known writer said, "God uses the family as a timeless platform throughout history to display His glory to all generations. And every member in the family has a unique role to portray the heart of God." Within this statement lies the great responsibility to shape the minds, hearts, and souls of our precious children. We must teach them the ways of the Lord and let them know that they are special in His sight. As parents, we can only give to them what we have been given. So, it is up to us to gain as much knowledge as possible to influence them to develop what is already inside of them.

Some have asked, "Have you and your husband ever had a difference in opinion raising your children?" Yes. A. D. and I, just like any other couple, were individuals who entered a relationship with a different set of experiences. We faced such turmoil with our two boys who passed away. Beyond that, we realized how important it was for us to communicate with each other so that we would be on the same page where our other children were concerned. My husband was off working many times. He had eleven mouths to feed, so he couldn't afford to stay at home and raise the children, so much of it was left up to me. I just prayed and did my best. Thank God A. D. had good jobs that showed him favor.

With our last four children, Kevin, Anita, Delphine, and Steve, we learned that we could allow them to have a measure of freedom and yet please God. We took family vacations, went out to dinner, and taught them the ways of the Lord. They could play sports, go to parties, and participate in school events. Steve even won, "Best Dancer" in high school. Delphine remembers us taking them to McDonald's to enjoy Big Macs while taking that opportunity to teach them proper etiquette. I even went as far to allow Anita to ditch class when she was in high school. I told her to simply call me when she felt the need to do so. I wanted her to know that she was safe, and I wanted her to trust me.

Kevin wanted to play music, and A. D. and I wanted him to go into a field that we felt was more secure. So, we went down to a computer school, enrolled Kevin, bought books, and gave him the start date. He never stepped foot in that school because he knew what he wanted to do. He worked a short time at a job and decided to quit and take his retirement and buy recording equipment. The rest is history. He is now a Tony Award-nominated and Grammy Award-winning musician. I believe this type of freedom gave my last four children space to grow in positive directions.

A. D. and I were making more money than we had ever made, we lived in a house bigger than we had ever lived in, and we began to build a legacy for our family to enjoy. We were mature, we were more educated than we had ever been before, and we had learned the importance of communication and commitment. So, life was much easier with our last four children. I realized that I was a perfectionist with my first three children—Urie, Gloria, and Arthur. I wanted everything to be in order. And I was too lenient on Billy and Lorell; I allowed them to set their own boundaries. But with God's help, I struck a balance with the last four. As I learned better, I applied it to our lives.

LESSONS I LEARNED WORKING IN LA JOLLA, CALIFORNIA

I used every opportunity to gain knowledge. I always say that you can learn from anyone you're around. I learned a great deal working in La Jolla, California. Most of my clients were White upper-class families; they could afford around-the-clock nursing, cooks, and house maids. I saw how they treated their children, like little princes and princesses. They allowed them to be themselves, to have an opinion, and to be open. They didn't keep telling them, "No," "Stop that," "Don't do that," or "Get out of grown folks' business." They allowed them to explore and be comfortable around adults. I saw them eating cheese sandwiches and soup for dinner. I had never seen anyone eat a sandwich at that time of day—that was news to me. I always thought I had to cook a full, heavy meal, for it to be called dinner. I saw how much energy they had even when they were eighty or ninety years old. Their diet played a huge role in their lifestyle, and I started adopting their lifestyle in my own family. I learned a lot about raising my last four kids that way. I don't believe one way of raising my kids was better than the other; it was just different.

Breaking the Trend

When I was growing up, children were not esteemed the way they are today. All what we did to educate ourselves, to learn the ways of the Lord, and the hardship we endured was to improve our family. We wanted our children to know the best of life; that's why we moved to California. We didn't want our children to be raised under the shadow of Jim Crow. We were young and full of ambition, so when we were told that the opportunities were endless in California, we packed up and went.

Both A. D. and I came from somewhat fragmented childhoods. So how would we come together and take the responsibility to raise children who would go on to impact the world? All parents have dreams for their children when they grow up, and I always said I needed my children's father to help me, so I was committed to making our relationship work. That was the only way I figured we could accomplish this goal.

I was careful to make sure that each child received some attention as an individual. They were all different, so they required different levels of attention. I was committed to teaching them to identify the strengths that were within them, so they could feel a sense of self-worth. To do that, I had to teach them not just man's principles alone but also God's principles. I had to make sure that they learned to access the unlimited power within to feel any self-worth. It was important for my children to know that they were great and that they can always expand and grow to be a greater person.

When I was growing up, Negroes, in my opinion, made two common mistakes with their children. First of all, in those days, skin color would sometimes divide families. They would educate the light ones and leave the black ones to the side. It's sad that our people did that, but it's the truth. I set it up in my heart that I was going to break the trend. I told the Lord that in raising my kids, I would never make a difference with skin color. And I didn't either! I never separated them, and I had kids all the way across the color palette. Steve was a very fair baby when he was born. For a long time, he was real light. He, Arthur, Delphine, Lorell, and Gloria were all light. My other kids, Urie, Billy, Anita, and Kevin, came out a little darker, but you ask them if I ever treated them differently. No, no, no—don't bring me that with my kids! I didn't care what the trend was. My children wouldn't be cursed by those silly ideas. I didn't allow people to hold those old laws over my children's heads; we've been redeemed.

Christ hath redeemed us from the curse of the law, being made a curse for us: for it is written, cursed is everyone that hangeth on a tree. (Gal. 3:13, KJV)

I need this generation to remember, you are not cursed by your complexion; you can't be cursed anymore. Jesus paid the price and that took away the curse, so nothing you've got is cursed. All those old wives' tales about the seventh of the seventh of the seventh and other stuff, that's gone! We are all a blessing from God. People made a lot of things bad luck for black folks in those days, and they didn't have no better sense than to pass all that mess down to their children. That's why we've got all these folks killing themselves and killing one another. Did you all know that we are the cause of some of that? Because when we teach our children wrong, they will turn around and teach their children that same way. And when you teach children, it's in them, good or bad. They believe it because momma or daddy said so. I learned years ago that my redemption was in the Bible. I was so glad to find out that we are not cursed because we are black; that's a lie from the pit of hell!

The second mistake was that Negroes in those days allowed other people to raise their children. I believe those ideas had a way of ruining children's lives. I witnessed it first hand with someone I was very close to. We all lived near each other. She was older than me, and we could have helped one another out. But she would fight day and night, cursing and carrying on. She was so jealous of her husband that it literally made her sick. You see, her mother had given her away, but it was for a good reason. Her mom had over twenty children, and she wanted some of them to be educated, so she picked my fair-skinned friend, the one who showed intellect, to be educated by her brother. Oh yes, she was nice and educated! I believe she finished high school, which was a great accomplishment in those days, but she was mentally off.

My friend could never understand why her mother gave her away. I remember she always asked, "Why did my mother give me away?" I don't know why parents didn't explain things to their children in those days. Her mom could have easily sat her down and said, "Honey, I have a lot of kids, and I am very poor. I don't have the money to put you through school, but my brother doesn't have children, so he has more resources to educate you and give you the opportunity to move forward in life, maybe even come back and help out the family." My good friend eventually lost her mind and had to be committed into the sanitarium. I perfectly understand that her mom was just following the trend. Desperately attempting to get out of poverty. It was popular to educate the light ones, those who showed promise. That's sad, but it's the truth.

That's what taught me that I wasn't ever going to give any of my kids away, no matter how many I had. You can do it for the best reason, but it does not necessarily make it any better for the child. Some may say, "I can't raise them. I can't sufficiently take care of them, so I'm going to give them away." Parents don't know it, but their love and limited resources can go farther than all the riches in the world.

To this day I tell children that they're great. I tell the children when I am speaking down at the church. They may not bit' mo pay me no attention, but I let the parents know that they may be raising the next president! Now you can put your foot on that statement because we have had a black president. They may be a doctor who will discover the next cure for cancer or some other disease. You don't know who you are raising, so that's the reason I tell them to be careful and don't just say, "You'll make it," without helping them. Give them all the help you can.

CHAPTER 10

Communication and Commitment Will Take You through All of Life's Cycle

A.D. and I celebrating our life together

Lower left to right: Lorell Sr., Ozell, A.D.,

Upper left to right: Urie Sr., Billy Sr., Kevin Sr.,
Gloria, Delphine, Anita, Steve Sr., Arthur Sr.

Definition of Communication

Webster's definition ~Communication \kə-ˌmyü-nə-ˈkâ-shən\ the act or process of using words, sounds, signs, or behaviors to express or exchange information or to express your ideas, thoughts, and feelings to someone else

Ozell's definition ~I simply say, "no one can read your mind!"

Definition of Love

I did not know in the beginning just how much it would entail for me to commit, and how important it was for me to learn how to properly communicate. I found out years later that it takes a lifetime of discipline to be successful. But the most important thing I learned was that if you can commit you can love, and that's what I wanted most of all, to love my family and they love me in return. But the question that may linger is, what is Love? According to the Bible, love has a definition all its own,

> "If I speak in the tongues of men and of Angels, but have not love, I am a noisy gong or clanging cymbal. And if I have prophetic powers, and understand all mysteries and all knowledge, and if I have all faith, to remove mountains, but have not love, I am nothing. If I give away all I have, and if I deliver up my body to be burned, but have not love, I gain nothing. Love is patient and kind; love does not envy or boast; it is not arrogant or rude. It does not insist on its own way; it is not irritable or resentful.
>
> It does not rejoice at wrongdoing but rejoices with the truth. Love bears all things, hopes all things. Love never ends. As for

prophecies, they will pass away; as for tongues, they will cease for knowledge, it will pass away. For we know in part and we prophesy in part, but when the perfect comes, the partial will pass away. When I was a child, I spoke like a child, I thought like a child, I reasoned like a child. When I became a man, I gave up childish ways. For now, we see in a mirror dimly, but then face to face. Now I know in part; then I shall know fully, even as I have been fully known. So now faith, hope, and love abide, these three; but the greatest of these is love" (1 Cor 13: 1–13).

Love, my friend, is the answer to the world's problems.

Root of Communication

The story of Adam and Eve is the perfect example of how damaging poor communication can be to a relationship. In the Garden of Eden, God communicated to Adam what not to do; and he told him what to leave alone. I believe if Adam had properly communicated the boundaries to Eve, she would not have eaten from the garden as God had instructed. Rather, Eve got her instructions from the serpent, which was the devil, the evil force (Gen. 3). The serpent was more successful in communicating the message to Eve than Adam. He was so successful that Eve turned around and convinced her husband to disobey as well. Just by communicating, the devil won in the end. Man sold out his birthrights and ours when he ate the forbidden fruit. This story shows the importance of effective communication. If Adam had been closer to his wife, the two of them together could have been more effective in resisting the serpent.

Communication entails more than just talking, you must show yourself to be a good listener as well. When two people are talking at the same time, it is not communication, and that is why arguing is so ineffective. If one waits until the other person is finished talking and intently listens, there is a chance that you will get greater clarity.

Mine and A. D.'s relationship suffered therefore; it was awkward for me to express my needs and desires to him. I clammed up early in life. I never learned how to sit down and communicate my feelings, because my dad treated us distant. I believe it was because of the stigma in our culture. Some fathers would molest their daughters, and at times fathers would create a regular sexual relationship between them and their daughters. And I believe my papa wanted to stay his distance to avoid getting attached to any stigma. But as a result, that may have caused me some of my anxiety when I got grown, I'm sure.

A. D. and I were married, and we had moved to Texas. I was a full-grown woman, but I yet missed my papa. I remember it well, I wrote him a long letter telling him how much I loved him and missed him. Do you know what he did? He wrote me back and told me, "Don't you ever write a letter like that again and send it to me!" That hurt my feelings so bad, I never shall forget how it felt for my papa, the man I loved so much and missed dearly, to scold me in that way. It was times such as these that I would clam up even more.

A. D. was like a cuddly bear, so to speak. He would just take me and hug me and tell me he loved me, and I'd say to him, "I love you too," I would say that lots of times, but it wasn't like I was comfortable saying it. I wasn't used to being hugged. I reckon it was because I wasn't cuddled and hugged when I was young, like I should have been. My grandmother loved me dearly, and I would catch hold to her coattail and go here and there, but I can never remember her cuddling me, so I held up a wall to my emotions.

CHAPTER 11

Remembering My Final Years With A.D.

(2013-2014)

A.D. preparing for his 90th birthday

Pure Love

I would often think that A. D. was just in the habit of saying "I love you." When I would get mad at him and threaten that I was going to do this or that, he would respond, "Well, I'm not, because I love you." That made me even angrier. Mrs. Ella Mae told me years ago that he said, "From the very first day I saw Ozell, I loved her, and I knew she was going to be my wife." I didn't know somebody could do that; it sounded impossible to me! I never believed that you could just look at a person and feel love. I'd never heard that. I found out that he wasn't kidding; he really did love me.

Neither my grandmother, dad, sisters or brothers loved me the way he did. Not only did he love me, he tried to look out and care for me. I felt very safe with him; we didn't have a lot, but I felt safe. It may sound simple, but I never had to worry about whether I was going to have a place to stay, because he was going to keep me with a place to stay, something to eat, and pretty well what I wanted, he would give it to me.

A. D.'s Illness

"I have to get out of this bed!" That's what the kids told me A. D. said when he heard I had been rushed to the hospital from what appeared to be a stroke. I realized that, little by little, I was losing control of one side of my body. The glass that I was holding slipped through my limp hand and fell to the ground. This news sent Him into a panic! He was lying in bed at the mercy of his deteriorating body. His mind had the determination of that thirteen-year-old boy across the fence, singing a cotton-picking tune, but his body was out of sync. A. D. said that it was his battle with Satan that left his skin sagging and his body frail. He didn't even have sufficient strength to stand up, much less to get out of bed. He told Anita that he had an encounter in a lucid dream,

> "He was being tossed around for days by that evil force. He fought with all his strength not to be overtaken. After every muscle in his body had been torn to shreds, he stood outside of his feeble body looking over at the park bench where Satan had left it lying, helpless and defeated. The battle was over!
>
> Just then, God went over to the body and did a thorough examination, and although my husband could not move a muscle, he wanted God to approve him as a good soldier. God came back with the verdict that, although his body was helpless to move, his spirit was found to be pure through and through."

But who was going to take care of his little barefoot country girl over in the hospital? He often told me that he wished I would go first, because he didn't think people would understand me the way he did.

Realizing my husband was Leaving Me

I stayed out of A.D.'s room in his last days, so there was a lot I did not know, and I did not want to know. I felt like if I stayed around, he would have held onto me. My presence would have put me on his mind, making him think of how he was going to take care of me and all that stuff. I would have been a hindrance to him, and I knew he wanted to go home to be with the Lord; I felt it.

That was the hardest thing I'd ever done in my life. Watching him wither away was painful. I would go out, get in the car, and in a daze, I would drive all day long. One day I almost ran off a cliff. The only way I knew it was a cliff was because the street ended, and my car stopped on the curb. I drove from one place to another, and then I would turn around and continue to wander around town. I don't know where all I didn't go. I was so confused.

I knew that death was a part of life, and I knew he was passing, but I didn't know how to handle it. I didn't want to be there. I didn't know anyone I could talk to, so it was very hard for me. I wanted him to go home in the victory, not just lie there and fade away, unable to eat, suffering from bedsores, and thank God he didn't experience those things. The doctors complimented the family on the superb way A. D. was cared for. Through all of this, our children each took four-hour shifts to ensure he had everything he needed.

A. D.'s Death

Can a heart actually break? I believe mine did. At 11:00 p.m. on November 3, 2014, A. D. passed away, and my heart broke in two. I almost died! A blood vessel had burst in my eye, I had a mini-stroke, and now it felt as if I was breathing through a narrow straw. My air supply was slowly being cut off. I walked through the house wheezing and panting for my next breath. For the first time ever since I had started my walking program, I had no energy or motivation to go to Chollas Lake. Anita said, "Mom, those don't even sound like words that can come out of your mouth, that you don't have the desire to walk." I told her that my energy seemed like it was so low. I wanted to go walking, that's why I got up, but my body was too weak. I cried out to God, "Lord, help me! Whatever you allow me to do, I thank you."

God is good to me. I went to Chollas Lake and walked around one time. I had been so sick that I didn't think I would ever be able to go there again, and frankly after A. D. got sick, I was miserable trying; I just didn't have the will. My breathing got so bad that Anita and her husband Jay took me to the emergency room at Cedars-Sinai in Los Angeles. I was immediately admitted into the hospital from the emergency room. The EKG showed that my heart was not beating; it was merely fluttering. I was in heart failure. In an emergency procedure, Kevin watched as my cardiologist walked into the room, and without saying a word, he attached a 21G needle to a 50 ml syringe inserted it into my back and withdrew sixteen ounces of fluid off my lungs. This saved my life.

Once the emergency settled, the doctor came back into the room, sat down, and looked me straight in the eyes and asked me, "Do you want to live?" At that time, I began to reflect over my life. I mean, how can I put a lifetime into perspective lying right there in a hospital bed? I thought about it. My strong, handsome papa and Grandma Emma, the only momma I ever knew, were both silenced by brain strokes. MaeLee and Alee were both dead. Frank had a tragic death; he was burned alive in a house fire. They said he screamed a long time trying to get out, but he couldn't. Alvernia died of heart failure. So, it was just Lonnie Jr. and I left from my childhood family. Two of my sons, Billy Ray and Lorell, died five months apart, and now A. D. was gone.

The real question at this point was that what do I have to live for? I had done just about everything that one human being can do. I had loved from the depths of my soul. I had tasted the sweet savor of life and the bitter, poisonous plant of hate and racism. I had gone through the emotional pain associated with great loss and physical pain of diseases. I had to wonder, "What is my life saved for? Who still needs me to be here?" Sometimes my family can't imagine how sad I feel, but God does. Boy, does he know, because I cry and tell him all about it. I had suffered so much, but I fought to stay alive, because after A.D. passed I wanted to give up and die right along with him. But, I thought about my kids. How would they survive after losing two parents within such a short period of time?

I concluded right there in that hospital bed that I still had a will to live, and that I was facing the ultimate test of faith and tenacity. For me to be still living was confirmation that God was not finished with me yet. I was confident that God had more work for me to do. Despite all of this, I am blessed to still have the health to accomplish all that God has placed on my heart for his people. Hallelujah! Glory to God. I told the doctor, "I will live and not die."

A Peace that Passes Understanding

I have peace because I know what A. D. stood for, I run across his scriptures now. I know what that man stood for, and it was the Word of God. It is for that reason I say that I believe he was at peace with God. Another thing I know—I know for sure—that he loved me. He might not have always acted right, and I'm not saying he was perfect, but I know one thing: that man loved me, and he always let me know that. I told him why I stayed with him. I said, "A. D., you know what? I can feel your love. Seem like I could just feel it."

For My Glory

I had prayed night and day for relief, and now God's word was becoming clearer to me when He said, "It's for my glory." Sometimes when the Spirit of the Lord comes, you don't always understand it right away. But as you go on, just watch him work. And when you watch him work, guess what? You are going to say, "Oh, that's what he was up to. That's what God was doing." Because the Bible says,

"And we know that all things work together for good to them that love God, to them who are called according to his purpose" (Rom. 8:28).

It didn't say that the things happening were good; it said it's "for my good." Somewhere down the line, they are working together. There are so many things that I didn't understand then that I understand now.

When the Spirit of the Lord spoke to me, I was walking down my hall, and I looked into the room where my husband was lying in the bed. His body seemed like it was just drying up and withering away. And I began to cry and tell God, "I don't understand what's going on." I said, "He's just lying there. He's not going home, and neither is he being healed." I wasn't questioning God; I just wanted to know from him what was going on so that I could get a little comfort. I went into his room to feed him, and as I started back out of the room, the Spirit of the Lord spoke to me, just like there was a person standing right there. It said, "It's for my glory. It's for my glory." So, when Anita said that the enemy had thrown his body and left it for dead, but God examined it and said that he was pure through and through, that gave me a confirmation, and it comforted me. It still wasn't easy, but I made it through. I was comforted that God got the glory out of his death some way or another. I don't know, but God does.

OZELL YOU'RE IN THE REAL WORLD NOW

I was faced with leaving the family home. The place where fifty-eight Thanksgiving dinners had been prepared, were the joyful screams of children on Christmas morning filled the house, and where our family sat around the living room furnace on those rare chilly mornings. The home that marked the beginning of us raising our last four children Steve, Delphine, Anita, and Kevin. I had to wrap my mind around this reality. I had to move on! Boy, how do I do that? I was only a teen when I married A. D., and I went from Papa's house to A. D. and went to having kids right away, so I had never lived alone. Ever!

God is awesome, because I pray, and he truly gives me the answers. It was December 2015, and I was getting ready to go into my second holiday season without A. D. My good friend Barbara Hayes sent an article that would change the way I thought about my future forever. It was called "Deposit Good Memories."

> "The article told of a man whose wife had died after seventy years. He was moving to a small place because he wasn't going to keep his house any longer, and somebody asked him, "You haven't seen your new room yet, have you?" (Because it was a small place where he was going to live in. Like one day I probably will.) "It doesn't matter; that doesn't have anything to do with it," he replied. "Happiness is something you decide on ahead of time. Whether I like my room or how the furniture is arranged doesn't depend on how I feel. It's how I arrange my mind."

That encouraged my heart. He was going to a place that was less than what he had enjoyed with his mate, and yet he was satisfied. He had arranged his mind to accept that, whatever was there, he was going to be happy. "I've already decided to love it," he said. "It's a decision I make every morning when I wake up. I have a choice: I can decide to spend the day in bed recounting the difficulties I have had with the parts of my body that no longer work or I can get out of bed with a thankful attitude for the ones that work and for the things I do."

You know, beloved? I did that this morning, now you can believe it or not! I didn't say it just like him, but I said to myself, "There are many things I used to do that I can't do now," but I got on my knees and reminded the Lord of all the things I was grateful for. I could run out of time telling him how grateful I am for what he has given me. I can walk, I can talk, I can even fix my own breakfast, and I can take my own baths. That is a blessing! For that and so much more, I give God the glory. I will make up in my mind that I will get up each morning in the spirit of gratefulness.

I make up in my mind that I will get out of bed just being thankful. Anybody in the house can hear me early in the morning glorifying and magnifying God.

Anita told me, "Yes, Mom, I do hear you, and it is a spiritual pleasure to listen. Sometimes I get up and sit at your door in silence, or I cry, pray, and magnify God with you." She went on to say, "I have asked God to please teach me how to pray like that, how to get up each morning with thanksgiving."

I told her, "Well, the older you get, the more you have to be grateful for," although I've always been grateful! When I was ten years old, I was just as grateful as I am now. I just didn't have as much to be grateful for. I think I was a chosen vessel of the Lord, I really do. I believe when my mother birthed me into the world, those heavenly tongues that she spoke could have been her way of dedicating me—I don't know.

But I first start out being thankful for the gift of the day. How God saw fit to heal my eyes, because I've had real problems with pain and discomfort. And how I can yet see without glasses and even drive. Second, I bring up a happy memory that's been tucked away. Sometimes I giggle and talk to people about things that A. D. did and how he responded to it. And you know what? That's just like a bank account. Well, it's more valuable than a bank account.

Miss Casey, a woman I cared for years ago when I was doing home nursing, shared with me something that I held on to all these years. She said her key to living a full life as she got older was to bring up beautiful memories of her traveling. She said, "Ozell, it's in my memory, and I can view it whenever I want to feel pure happiness."

Now, when I can't get out and go nowhere, it's raining, or I got a cold and can't get outside, guess what? I can just sit in this house and think of so many memories. I begin to make a withdrawal. There are days I could be looking at television and hear sound of child's laughter; it takes me to the scene of my two boys Billy Ray and Lorell running across the field toward school, one in kindergarten, and the other one in first grade. Taking them across the street and telling them to catch hands and be careful, to look out for one another. Or, I can smell hot biscuits cooking, and it reminds me of my family, all eleven of us, sitting around the kitchen table on Saturday morning. I would bake ten cans of biscuits, a whole box of Cream of Wheat, a pound of butter, and two gallons of milk. All I'm saying is, good memories can shift your mood.

Third, I free my heart from hatred. I pray for my enemies. I tell the Lord, "If I have any? They need you! They won't be able to find you as long as they hate." Fourth, I free my mind from worry. I live simply, and I give thanks for what I already have. Fifth, as God give to me, I give to others. I am giving more than I was when A. D. was alive. I have cleaned out closets and given away more than I ever thought I would. And sixth, I expect less and accept more. Just believe you are going to get less from people, starting with your own family, and accept more. Whatever the action of people is, let it be between them and God.

I thank God, I never feel lonely. My days are filled, and I constantly restructure my life. I get up and get out. I honestly have a lot of faith. I have faith that was once delivered to the saints. The Bible says,

"Beloved, when I gave all diligence to write unto you of the common salvation, it was needful for me to write unto you, and exhort you that ye should earnestly contend for the faith which was once delivered unto the saints" (Jude 1:3)

And why I say this is because, if I didn't have faith, I couldn't make it like I do. I have faith that things will be better the next day. You know why? Because God promised that to me! When I cry, I am mostly giving praise and thanksgiving.

And finally, I have learned that victory is in holding my peace. If I hold my peace and let the Lord fight my battle, victory shall be mine. Since I have said less and prayed more, I really have been victorious. The scripture reads,

"The Lord shall fight for you, and ye shall hold your peace" (Exod. 14:14)

CHAPTER 12

Ozell's Final Thoughts

(2016)

As I read through this memoir, I sat for some time with tears tickling the corners of my eyes. Thinking back over the years, these stories have aroused feelings that I thought were long gone. As with most people, I've encountered abundant joy, achieved great accomplishments, and experienced grief beyond human understanding, which I have succumbed to at times; I'm human.

But now, I am celebrating my golden years on this great earth, and I am still basking in the glory of God. The truth is, as I grow older, I feel wiser. I feel like this is the time when I can be fully trusted and can fully trust. This is by far my most precious season in life; I believe I have captured its true meaning. I've learned great lessons along the way. I know how to be a better me, a better Ozell. Others can profit from my life experiences, positive and negative. I can't leave anything out: the pitfalls, the mountains, and just plain living.

This is a time when I can make a difference in others' lives. I see the value in living to help someone else. The experiences that I have had in the past, I profit from them. I've learned how to be a good wife, live a better life for God, and be a better mother. When I was young, there was a spark of genius in my dreams, and I worked diligently to reach them. Now when I realize that most of my time is behind me, the spirit of peace and joy overcomes me. I invite others to stand on my shoulders to look back and celebrate the past. While there, I also invite them to rise to their tippy-toes and peek into the future. When I think of how I am giving my family this wealth of memories for the future, something for their children to look back on, I rejoice, and my heart sings, "How Great Is Our God!"

The Saddest Day of My Life and My Greatest Joy

Anita asked to describe the happiest and saddest days of my life. I didn't have to think about it, because those emotions sit on opposite ends of my heart spectrum. The saddest day was when Senior died. I couldn't understand how a precious life like his could leave so soon. But my and A. D.'s greatest joy, aside from accepting Christ in my life, was when Urie was born. We felt like he was our precious gift from God. It was the joy that I had never felt before.

What This Book Did for Me

I was asked to describe what this book did for me. I believe it released something. There was something bottled up inside of me, and I didn't understand how to get rid of it. I would hear other people say how they released it and became mentally balanced, how they became so happy just by writing. I had kept all these records. As I thought of things, I would write them down.

In the foreword, Anita said that she found little notes around the house here and there. She thought she was finding them. What she didn't know was that I strategically placed different things in her path so that she would find them. I have done this down through the years. I knew how curious my children were, so I satisfied her curiosity with pieces of nuggets about myself. I told her, "It was in hopes that it would acquaint you with who I was because y'all never sat down and listened to what I had to say. I understand that you were kids. Your dad's life was on a big screen, and that was who you looked up to, and that's fine. I wanted you to look at him. I taught you to look up to him, and I encourage y'all to keep looking at him. He was a fine man. He was a man of God who loved the Lord and prayed." But I thought, not as jealousy, but I simply said to myself, "None of my kids really know me." People only knew who my husband presented me as.

My granddaughter, Love, brought it to mind first when she was studying at Saint John's University in New York. She needed something for her class, so I sent her a video. Then my other granddaughters: Toy, Dorenda, and Kaira began to ask me about myself. My granddaughter Felicia even bought me a book where I only needed to answer the questions. It started me to thinking, "Maybe I'll write a book about myself." That's when I started writing.

My Greatest Life Lesson

My greatest life lesson was not abandoning my marriage and not aborting the mission to become the best mother I could be. I really thought I wanted to at times because I felt like I couldn't handle it; I felt so insufficient. But when I thought about my children and what I would have done to them, I thank God that I had enough sense to stay throughout my illnesses. That would have been the greatest mistake in my life. If I had left, I would have regretted it and spent an entire life attempting to make it right. If I had left my husband with the children, he would have eventually moved on; he would have kept growing and maybe even gotten remarried. That's what people do. But my children would have stopped growing on some level. If I had left, I would have suffered because leaving breaks a chain of confidence with your kids, and once you are out, it is hard to get back in; you put such doubt in their heart. Some may ask, "How did you learn this lesson when you didn't actually leave?" I've learned from others who did leave, and I watched how they suffered as a result.

I want my children to know that I only wanted to leave because my heart was heavy with depression and my body racked with pain; it had nothing to do with them. I was so weak that I could not do anything for my family, and I was mean because my body was not well. I didn't feel like I was of value, and I didn't feel worthy of letting my family take care of me. I never had a mother to let me take care of her; nobody taught me that! So, I didn't know how to relax and enjoy the luxury of someone taking care of me. I really wished I did! I now realize how important it is to allow your children to see you taking care of your loved ones, because they will then know how to take care of you when you are in need.

I have fled from the pain of loss throughout my entire life, but there is a clear indication that it still lingers in that deep space; the pain has been woven into the fabric of my being. But with the spiritual armor that I have collected over the years, I have learned how to suspend my sorrow, hold it at bay. I've learned to dry my tears so that I could care for myself and others who needed me.

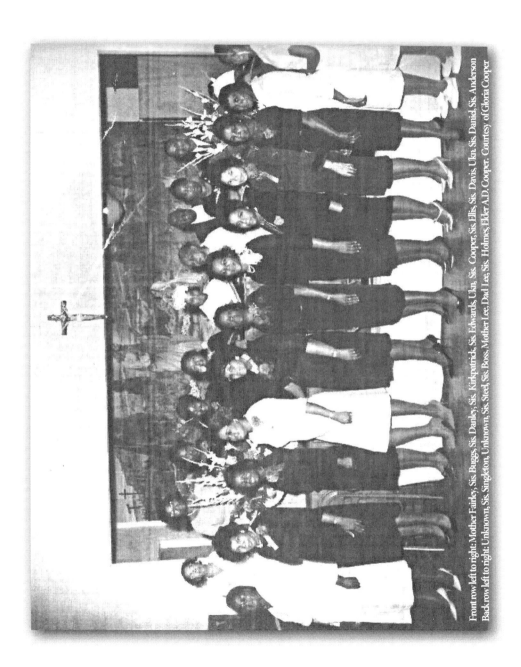

Front row left to right: Mother Fairley, Sis. Buggs, Sis. Danley, Sis. Kirkpatrick, Sis. Edwards, Ulan, Sis. Cooper, Sis. Ellis Sis. Davis, Ulan, Sis. Daniel Sis. Anderson

Back row left to right: Unknown, Sis. Singleton, Unknown, Sis. Steel, Sis. Boss, Mother Lee, Dad Lee, Sis. Holmes, Elder A.D. Cooper. Courtesy of Gloria Cooper

Left to right bottom: Arthur, Kevin, Billy (upper), unknown person, Anita, Steve (upper) Delphine, Lorell upper A.D. Back Left: Ozell, Mrs. Ella Mae, Mr. Joe, Mother Craig, Gloria, Abraham.

My family with mother Craig when they were small

Distinguished Service Award
86th Holy Convocation
Church of God In Christ International Sunday School Department

presented to

Ozella Cooper

For outstanding service as a teacher in
"The World's Largest Sunday School"
Sunday, November 14, 1993

Elder J.W. Macklin
In'l Sunday School Superintendent

Missionary Gloria Smith
Int'l Field Representative

Bishop L.H. Ford, Presiding Bishop

I was impressed that I kept so many people interested in my Sunday school class at the International Convocation. There must have been over 100 people in attendance in that class. I enjoyed it.

What I've Learned from My Seventy Years in the Church

I have seen many bishops come into office, state mothers come and go. I have seen blinded eyes opened; that happened in my church! I have seen lame people walk. I have seen legs lengthen where one was longer than the other. I've heard of cancer being spit up and tumors delivered like babies. And I myself have been a living miracle, being healed from malaria with no defect as far as I know. I remember hearing of my grandmother going to the meeting in Memphis. I would hear them talking about it. I don't know how they went, but my uncles and aunties and other ones did. They were church officials who knew the founding bishop of the Churches of God In Christ very well.

I remember Bishop C. H. Mason visiting Washington Chapel back when I was a child. But later in life, I saw him again because Looney Street was the mother church in Shreveport for the Western Louisiana Convocation, and Bishop White was the overseer. I was in the hospitality ministry that prepared the fellowship hall for the after-service meal. It was full of food; we had everything nice and guess what Bishop did. He got out of the car with all those brethren surrounding him, came in, and immediately dropped to his knees and began to pray. He then went to the dining table and began to eat. After eating he got right up and left. He was a man of few words but loads of prayer.

He preached one of his last messages at our church, House of Refuge, here in San Diego. He did the same thing: he got out of the car with all the brethren surrounding him, walked through the doors of the church, and fell to his knees and prayed, and then he got up, preached, and left without saying a word.

What was funny was that there was a minister at our church who tried to emulate him. He got on his knees and prayed, he got up and preached his heart out, and then he simply walked out the door without saying a word to anybody—he got in his car and left. The funny part about it was that he forgot and left his wife and children at church. He was gone, and his family had to find a way home. We laughed about that for a good while!

Bishop Mason was simply a praying man whom God gave a vision to, and he just carried it out. That's why it's essential that we pray because God will place the vision directly inside of us. But it is more important to get up and do something once you've prayed. We always felt so honored to be in the bishop's presence. I feel just as honored today when I am in Bishop McKinney's presence. He is a humble, anointed leader who has great concern for God's people. He has conquered so much and is yet doing a great work for God, and I pray for him daily.

Today's church is a little different, but I want my family to know something about the old church. You may never hear that old saint in the corner, covered with the Holy Ghost, shout out, "It's like fire, huh! Shut up in my bones!"

That's why I allowed my private, most intimate conversations with God to be released. It is so you, my family, will never forget the sound of heavenly tongues. It is so that you will turn to them when you wish to enter the secret place of the Most High, and so that you will learn to speak them as the Holy Spirit gives utterance,

"Follow after charity and desire spiritual gifts, but rather that ye may prophesy. For he that speaketh in an unknown tongue speaketh not unto men, but unto God: for no man understandeth him; howbeit in the spirit he speaketh mysteries" (1 Cor. 14).

If I were to put this book into one message, I would say, "Pray. God has the answer, and he will give it to you." Prayer has been the glue that has kept my life together. I believe I was born into prayer. When I was told that my mom was speaking in tongues as she delivered me, I truly believe that was her intimate conversation with God about me. In my imagination I think, "What could she have been possibly saying? I don't know! I've only heard bits and pieces about her, but I was exposed to her mother's prayers. My siblings didn't hang on to her coattail, hear her praying, and see her fasting and afflicting herself before the Lord the way I did. And when you fast, that's sho'nuff what you're doing.

After a short while living a life of sin, I caught the mantle; it's a wonderful thing! I believe that's why I'm yet alive. God has just caused me to soar because of my prayer life. I've overcome many things because I love to pray. Mother Nash saw fit to appoint me to the position of state prayer chaplain, and I don't take the position lightly. I first consult God for his direction in my life, and then I pray for God to give me what the saints of God need to hear so that they will be encouraged to keep on keeping' on. I've held many positions in the Church before I came to San Diego but none of them has excelled the position of state chaplain of Second Ecclesiastical Jurisdiction. It is the greatest auxiliary I've served on. I relish the memory of Mother Nash saying, "The Women's Convention is not on until Sister Cooper get here to pray us in." It wasn't that I was important, it meant that the Holy Spirit used me to set the spiritual tone. God just used me to open things up. I would start out saying, *"I will bless the Lord oh my Soul and all that is within me bless His Holy Name. For he has done great things. You ought to stand to your feet and thank God for His many blessings. Bless the name of Jesus!"*

And we would have a Holy Ghost good time!

TRUE LIBERATION

Some of my negative experiences were difficult to share in this book. But I realized that they were life-shaping experiences. That's the balance: negative experiences brought out positive traits. Beloved, when God brings you out of all of life's turmoil, you must be careful not to play with God. You should run to him and tell him how much you magnify him.

I have learned that one soul who needs Christ is more important than thousands who already know him and are just waiting to be renewed. You know, because Matthew 18:12 reads,

> *"How think ye? If a man has a hundred sheep, and one of them be gone astray, doth he not leaves the ninety and nine, and goeth into the mountains, and seeketh that which is gone astray?"*

You never know who may be in that group who really needs to know about God and his love. I don't take any opportunity for granted. I witness to folks all over the city, and sometimes they just look at me. At times I give them the plan of salvation right there in Sunday school because I feel like they may have been in church all their life and still don't know the plan of salvation. How sad would it be for me to go before God and have him say, "You know what? You taught all those people, and I did not hear you give them a chance to come to me!" So, I just blare it out right in the middle of class.

I used to witness to my children right here in the house. I figured they may not remember what they learned in church. When Billy Ray and Lorell were acting up, boy, I would witness to them just like they were strangers. I witnessed to my oldest child right outside in my front yard. The Holy Ghost said, "Go out there and witness to him," and that's just what I did. I went out there, and he just looked at me. It was like he said, "Momma, did you know that you raised me?" I told him flat, "I have to know that you know that Jesus died for you." Every mother has the responsibility to be a spiritual guide to her children. How else will they know? They will follow someone and believe in something—it may as well you and Christ.

I have always told my kids, "If something happens to me, and God takes me home, keep your life going." If you want to make me happy and proud, don't give up on life; continue to live. If you're doing church work, keep on doing church work! If you are traveling, keep on traveling! Doing business? Don't stop! Always remember that you are the best thing that ever happened to you because God made you!

Remember who you are and that there are some things that can't be taken away from you. Whatever attitude you have, whatever personality you have, God gave that to you, and nobody can take it away. You can lose your car or your home, but it is impossible to lose what God gave to you. Sometimes I will be in my room reading my Bible for hours. I study about who I am in the eyes of God, and that's what makes me come out of that room boasting! God has given me the courage to fight, and I always have. I pray the way I do so that when I exit my room and face the fiery darts, I can do it with power and grace. If I couldn't see it in the Bible, I wouldn't say it.

I urge you, my loved ones, to get back to nature. Take a part of who you are, and guard it with your life. Don't be so consumed with the material things that you lose touch with who you are. The best way to live your life is to enjoy it wherever you are. Be where you are: married, not married; job, no job; money, no money—whatever situation you find yourself in, be content. First Timothy 6:6–7 reads,

"But Godliness with contentment is great gain. For we brought nothing into this world, and it is certain we can carry nothing out" (KJV).

I learned that principle through experience. I was going to wait until my children grew up to start doing this or that. But if you learn how to enjoy life where you are, you will have won life, and an abundant one at that. I learned it, but I learned it later in life. Yet it wasn't too late for me to enjoy my life. That's why I'm saying it to y'all: don't sit and wait; don't put off your life for your kids or anybody else. I'm telling you what I know, sho' as my name's Ozell. Live each day simply for the joy of it. Yes, you will go through things. I say, go through it and let it go! Don't hold on to it and carry it around.

Colossians 2:6–7, "*Let your roots grow down into him, and let your lives be built on him. Then your faith will grow strong in the truth you were taught, and you will overflow with thankfulness.*"

Advice to This Generation and Beyond

I am just determined to keep myself nailed down, because you must keep yourself anchored. With all the things that go on in this world, you must know that God will bring you through. It is going to take discipline to maintain yourself, to keep on living. I tell my children it takes courage to live. When the wind is blowing every which-a-way, you are going to have to seek God's answer for yourself. You can't please people. I don't do what anybody tells me to do; I seek God for my answer. You can hate me if you want. I have told my children, "If you don't like it, I can't help it. I'm not here to satisfy you, I'm not here to be your friend, and I'm sure not here to be your enemy. I'm here to help you with God's help." That's my mission!

Before I came to know Christ, I didn't know where the patience would come from, and I didn't know where the discipline would come from, because I had never raised children before. You mean I'm going to raise a child at seventeen, eighteen, and nineteen years old? Where did I get patience and discipline from? It had to be God. I wasn't perfect, but I did my best. Over the years, I have enjoyed my children, grandchildren, great-grandchildren, and great-great grandchildren. Beloved, I need you to know that God did not give your children to you, he gave them through you. This means, they are not your children, they are God's children for you to enjoy. You have a responsibility to nurture, protect, raise, and teach them. Most importantly, you are to spread God's goodness through them.

God has done us like he did the children of Israel. We find that God born them out to be a representative for him. That was his purpose for them. God wanted his name to be great among them. They were to show his goodness throughout the generations. So, when you are going through stressful times with your children, remember that they are not yours to keep. That doesn't take the responsibility away from you to raise them. But it does give you the permission to let them go into the world to live out God's purpose for their lives.

CHAPTER 13

God Answering My Prayers to See
My Mom, Josie Glover-Greer

When I moved to San Diego, California, Urie had just gotten his driver's license and bought a car, and I asked A. D. if Urie could take me on a road trip to Sacramento to visit my grandfather Steve, whom I had never seen before, but had heard so much about.

My father told me my grandfather's address when I was just a child, and it always stood out in my mind. He lived at 420 T Street for many years. Urie and I took off for Sacramento. I can remember so well Grandpa Steve's great big house, it was just about downtown. When we arrived I first met my step-grandmother and my aunt Alpha Omega. Grandma Betty had passed on. I told my step-grandmother my story about I never saw my grandfather and I came to Sacramento to see him. She said, "Well, baby, your grandfather is at the park." In those days, people didn't direct you to where you wanted to go; they just described landmarks. On the way to the park, we spotted my grandfather walking home. I knew who he was because he was the spitting image of my papa. It was just like seeing my dad in an old body.

He was walking just as peer as an aristocrat. Straight and tall, his head up with an air of confidence. Urie and I got out of the car and started walking alongside of him and talking. He was listening to me but looking at Urie. He was so elated with my son because we did not have many boys in the Greer family. All his children who lived around him were girls. He had my uncle and my dad, but they lived far away. So, he got busy getting acquainted with Urie. We walked a portion of the way home with him, and when we reached his front steps, I was going to help him climb them. He told me flat, "Get out the way, gal! I can climb these steps," so I stepped aside. We had a wonderful reunion once inside.

We talked about my dad, my uncle, my life, and as much as he knew about my mother. He didn't want to talk too much about her. He was displeased because of the early marriage between my mom and dad. And the life that my dad decided to live. I don't know the particulars about his relationship with my mother, but he didn't want to talk a lot about her. But I do remember him talking about my dad.

My auntie, Alpha Omega Greer was Papa's sister. We called her baby Auntie. You could tell she was family because she had the classic Greer trait: she was big boned, weighed about five hundred pounds, and crow's feet formed on the outside corners of her eyes when she laughed. She was one of the sweetest women I ever met. I had never met anyone who knew my mother as well as Alpha Omega Greer. Not only did she know my mother, but she had lived with her. So, I asked her, "Auntie, please describe my mother to me." I didn't tell her what I'd seen; I just let her make the description. She sat down and began look back through the dusty window of her mind and found the exact image that God had given to me in my dream when I was six years old. I thank God for her because nobody else had taken the time to give me that information. I reckon it didn't mean that much to her, but it meant so much to me. That is one trip I will remember forever. She lived in the basement of Grandpa Steve's home, and I sat at her feet and listened to her intently as she told me stories about my mother. She said my mom was a wonderful and humble person, and she loved God.

Urie and I wanted to spend the night, but my step-grandmother said she had no room. She had this great big house but no room. So, I called my first cousin Doris on my mother side and asked her to allow us to stay overnight with her. I found out that my step-grandmother was a bit cantankerous. She was not too friendly with my aunts as well. So, I didn't enjoy my stay as much as I wanted to, but we didn't plan to stay long anyway because I had to get back to A. D. and the other kids, and I believe Urie had a job at the time that he had to get back to. But I did plan a trip to go back.

I wanted to take all my children back. I kept touch with my aunts and cousins so that I could have connections there, because I wanted to spend more time with my grandfather; he was growing old. He was pretty close to ninety at that time. So, I planned that trip for my family to meet my grandfather. It was difficult for A. D. to get off work because he had so many children to support and he did not believe in welfare. No reflection on anyone, but he wanted to teach his boys a principle about working to support the family. Ha-ba-shae-de (holy tongues) glory to God! He wanted his boys to know that they can work and make a living for their family. So, he was not able to go with us, but I took all my children to Sacramento. I depended on Doris to help me. She was my best friend and cousin. We really loved one another and had been in touch since we were little girls.

Once again, I was not welcomed into my grandfather's home by my step-grandmother. I don't believe she had anything against me, and I didn't have anything against her. So, we stayed at Doris' house. She welcomed us. The next day or so we went to visit my grandfather. I wanted to get there before he got out of the house for the day, so I went early. I shall never forget that I told him about how I had cut my papa's hair for years. And believe it or not, he had me cut his hair. It was my pleasure that he trusted me on his hair. We talked more about his boys that he had not seen in years, since he left the South on his escape from the Jim Crow people in the 1930s. He never went back to the South, and they never made an effort to go out the West to see him.

So, I brought him up to date on my sisters and brothers and those he didn't know anything about. We talked and talked and talked. But out of all that talk, he never told me that he was a Holiness preacher. I don't know why. I talked about our church and A. D. being a minister. But he never opened his mouth. I was told that he went to the park every day and preached. I didn't go and hear him. I wished a many day I would have.

We planned a date to go out with my grandfather, so Urie drove us to the State Capital there in Sacramento. I was having the best time of my life standing there on the steps of the Capital holding on to my father's arm. I visited my grandfather for about three days before heading back to San Diego, but I had promised him that I would visit him again. But you know, soon after I returned home, my grandfather died. And with the amount of responsibility I had, I was not able to go to the funeral.

God Filling the Void for My Mom Josie Glover-Greer

All my life, I thought, "If I had my mother, the void would have been filled." I described it earlier as a "hole blazing through my heart." I would feel depression, but I could not put my finger on what was nagging me. But when I accepted Christ as my personal savior, I learned that even having a mother would not have been good enough to fill that void; the loneliness that I felt. God gave me the serenity that I had been looking for down through the years. He gave me a rich peace that passed all understanding; it was something that only Christ could give. Only Christ could fill that void, and I am so grateful for it. I held on to the scripture in 2 Cor. 5:17. It's true: I am that new creation.

I believe God showed me my mom when I was just a child. God saw fit to give me something to hold on to in my early years. I learned early in life not to let go of that vision; the way I saw her, I just held it in my heart. Then when I asked Auntie to describe her, and she gave me the exact vision I had in my dream, I was relieved, but I still felt that void.

GOD SETTING UP THE ATMOSPHERE

When Josie spoke those heavenly tongues as she delivered me, I believe she was setting up the atmosphere for me, way back then. The Holy Spirit was going before me, her baby, praying for me even up to this point in my life. The Bible speaks about how our fights are not carnal:

> *"For we wrestle not against flesh and blood, but against principalities, against powers, against the rulers of the darkness of this world, against spiritual wickedness in high places"* (Eph. 6:12, KJV).

We do not have to wrestle. When we can't see our way, the Holy Spirit makes our way through principalities, power, and the rulers of the darkness of this world, and against spiritual wickedness in high places. But it takes prayer and fasting. It can cut through the atmosphere. It can break it up like the clouds on a sunny day. The Holy Spirit can do it, but you must stand on those principles.

I believe that, knowing somewhere in her spirit that she wouldn't be here for me, Josie was setting up the atmosphere for me to have a long and prosperous life. That is the power of speaking in tongues; it is truly a personal language between you and God. The seed was planted in me and delivered by Josie, then nurtured by Grandma Emma. Josie birthed some things into this generation through me. As she delivered me, she delivered God's promises to this generation. God knew that I would be a lifetime witness for Him, that I would proclaim His name through all the earth.

I have come to believe that God rescued me from years of suffering and heartache when He came into my life at such a young age. One of the thoughts that came to me was that, when I prayed for God to show me Josie, He honored that—not only in the vision I had as a six-year-old but also, He has shown me her in me. I am she; I am Josie. There are so many parts of Josie that are stamped into the very essence of my being. For that and so much more, I am grateful. Josie died so that I might live and declare the works of the Lord. Oh hallelujah, bless His name! She died so that an entire generation would live to tell the world about a God who will deliver them in times like these.

Now I wake up and pray those same prayers that Josie prayed, and Josie prayed those same prayers that Grandma Emma prayed. Who will pray now? Who can I depend on to pray for our generations when God calls me home? Who can I pass the mantle on to? As I have said before, I have been faithful to God down through the years, and one thing is for sure: if you are faithful, you can depend on God's promises. It is never too late.

I have come to accept that some questions will forever remain unanswered, and I am grateful that today my dream has become a reality; this book is proof that Josie's girl never gave up on her dream. I have also come to appreciate the reality that my mom, Josie, gave me the most important step of all, my first step. She birthed me into the world; God did the rest.

If dreams die, they are like a broken-winged bird that cannot fly.

~LANGSTON HUGHES

EPILOGUE

Over the past couple of years, I have read hundreds of pages that my Mother wrote about her life. I invested many hours transcribing, dictating, interviewing, and performing supplemental research. I filed away handwritten notes that I found around the house, eavesdropped on telephone calls, and secretly recorded her singing and praying. Year after year my mother's words just danced around in my head.

But the closer I came to the end of this project, the further away it appeared. It seemed as if information was surfacing everywhere! Folding decades of a life into a neat box is truly more than I can describe. It was as if there were one million pieces that needed to be put together, sort of like a puzzle. I transcribed Mom's vernacular, raw thoughts, emotions, and thinking, all to portray her in the truest sense. It really was one of the greatest literary challenges I've ever faced. She is so interesting to listen to. I have never met anyone who told stories with such detail, inflection, and fire! For years, through Mom's eyes I have had the pleasure of thinking about love and all its escapades.

Love so adoring that it causes a winding maze, a maze so beautifully complicated that only a spiritual road map can locate the exit.

I lived through the stories of her and Dad meeting, marrying, and starting a family. The stories of them carving their footprints into the old Southwest in search of "the world of opportunity" that they had heard so much about. I imagined them traveling across country, looking out the car window at the passing scenery as the countryside gave way to small towns and small towns turned into the big city. My parents had traded the pine-shaded roads of Louisiana for Texas Mountains that shimmered in the sun like a mirage. In my mind's eye, I see tumbleweeds blow across the wide, empty highways of New Mexico. Highways that seemed to stretch into eternity. I see them look out in amazement at the Joshua trees of Arizona that seemed to be worn to their gray bones. And the twisting canyons of El Centro that finally opened up, to crashing waves that calmed down on the edges of the enthralling sands of San Diego. It was official: they had traded the star-filled skies of the South for the hot and glorious sun of San Diego. I always thank my mom and dad for having the courage to leave their comfort zones in the South, to pursue their dreams in California.

If I had to sum up my mother's life in one word, it would have to be "love." Her entire life has been absorbed in it. The undying love she has for her mom, Josie, who wisped past her for a brief six weeks. Mom, there is no doubt in my mind that Josie loves you and has guided you through these years. The love Grandma Emma showed when she blessed my mother with the treasure of witnessing her pray, fast, and place the family on the throne of grace. The commitment that Mom showed our father by holding on to the powerful grip of love for nearly seventy-three years.

My heart synchronized with my mom's in December 2014, one month after Daddy passed away. That deep and undying love that she was feeling penetrated from her heart into mine. I cried as I watched her walk through the house fighting back the tears that were so necessary. She was remembering what had seemed to escape everyone else's mind: The greatest loss of love that she would ever experience with Dad, triggered sad memories of her two sons Lorell and Billy. I thought, "If she would allow those floodgates to open, it would be a cleansing ceremony so great that it would seal her heart with the healing balm that she needs to roll through this holiday season in the lap of Love."

Mom, may I say you taught your kids to be confident, adventurous, and free to move to the edge of life. *That's love!* You taught us to be comfortable under the bright lights on the world stage. *That's love!* We were taught to think highly of ourselves and others. *That's love!* You challenged us to meet our highest self and show courage in the face of opposition. *That's love!*

Hey, people! Do you think that we are safe just for safety's sake? Do you think that we excel and are in good health just for the sake of the word? Do you think that we live abundant lives and overcome obstacles just because we are that good? Do you think that we have healthy families because we are favored in the natural selection process of life? Don't fool yourselves, for it is the fervent prayer of our mom, the cries from the depths of her soul, the petitioning to God for the cares of this world to be taken off our shoulders. That's the reason!

Silver and gold, we have not, but we do have the power and protection to make huge dents in this world. We would be remiss if we don't. The prevailing prayers that Mom, her grandmother, and those prayer warriors in our ancestry who called our names even before we were a thought, are sustaining us. They prayed for us, they called us out by name, and they put us before the throne of Grace one by one.

When Mom instructed us to take a piece of ourselves and guard it with our lives, she spoke the summation of Ecclesiastes 1:

Everything Is Meaningless
The words of the Teacher, son of David, king in Jerusalem: "Meaningless! Meaningless!" says the Teacher. "Utterly meaningless! Everything is meaningless." What do people gain from all their labors at which they toil under the sun?

Generations come, and generations go, but the earth remains forever. The sun rises and the sun sets, and hurries back to where it rises. The wind blows to the South and turns to the North; round and round it goes, ever returning on its course. All streams flow into the sea, yet the sea is never full. To the place the streams come from, there they return again. All things are wearisome, more than one can say. The eye never has enough of seeing, nor the ear its fill of hearing.

What has been will be again, what has been done will be done again; there is nothing new under the sun. Is there anything of which one can say, "Look, this is something new"? It was here already, long ago; it was here before our time. No one remembers the former generations, and even those yet to come will not be remembered by those who follow them.

Wisdom Is Meaningless
I, the Teacher, was king over Israel in Jerusalem. I applied my mind to study and to explore by wisdom all that is done under the heavens. What a heavy burden God has laid on mankind! I have seen all the things that are done under the sun; all of them are meaningless, a chasing after the wind. What is crooked cannot be straightened; what is lacking cannot be counted.

I said to myself, "Look, I have increased in wisdom more than anyone who has ruled over Jerusalem before me; I have experienced much of wisdom and knowledge." Then I applied myself to the understanding of wisdom, and also of madness and folly, but I learned that this, too, is a chasing after the wind. For with much wisdom comes much sorrow; the more knowledge, the more grief. "(Eccles. 1 [NIV])

Everyone, rich or poor, seeks to know their purpose here on earth. These Holy Scriptures speak of the epiphanies that Solomon, the wisest and richest man to ever live, had at the end of his life. My mother, Ozell Greer-Cooper, has epitomized these same sentiments about what she has learned in her lifetime; after you have attempted to live out man's definition of success, there is only one answer to life's incomprehensible questions:

"Let us hear the conclusion of the whole matter: Fear God and keep his commandments: for this is the whole duty of man." (Eccles. 12:13 [KJV]

This is the mantra that I am committed to speaking as I pass down the oral and written history to my daughters; Anastaysia, Mishalay, Lailah, Love; and those who will come behind them. It is the foundation that I will stand on as I consider the future. I promise, Mom, that I will hide this word in my heart and allow it to become the essence of my being. It is because of these words that I am forever changed.

In the foreword, I said that I did not know why my Mother chose me to do this project. Now that I am approaching the end, it has become crystal clear. It wasn't to help her, it was for me to blossom. It was what I needed to know to complete my life. I needed to know the intricate details of her life so that I could fill in the gaps in my own. I needed to learn these lessons so that I could emerge from this project a more powerful woman of God, a more nurturing mother and grandmother, and a more empathetic sister, aunt, and friend. It was so that I could show more compassion than my humanness could contain. It all happened on this journey.

It's October 2017, and I am my mother's primary caretaker. We live in that small apartment that she spoke of in earlier chapters. Oh, how blessed I am to be under the same roof as this woman of God. She imparts wisdom daily. This morning she told me, "I guess you look at me and wonder, 'What's wrong with this lady? She used to get up and turn around, jump up, sit down with all the energy in the world.' Now you see me, and I'm barely putting one foot before the other. It sometimes takes hours for these bones to get going." She said, "My only desire is to do something to please the Lord."

Mom wept as she told me, "Sometimes I have to go in my room and cry after I tell my kids what God give me to say. Because one day I'm going home, and y'all can't say that you didn't know." If I may speak for our family, Mom, please tell us all what God has given to you. Give us the Living Word, because it causes us to grow in positive directions. This information that you have so graciously handed over to us is truly a priceless gift, and we will treasure it forever. I am confident that it will be a life-changing experience for anyone who picks up this book; it's historical, informational, visual, and a bit humorous at times.

My mother has felt the summer's heat under her feet, she has witnessed nature change its coat from stunning earth-toned leaves to a winter's carpet of snow, and she has felt the spring showers that display God's promise of rainbows; her life has come full circle. I look down the hall, and although her mind is razor sharp and she still has that youthful wit, the pain in her leg pushes her body slightly forward, and her feet never leave the floor as she shuffles toward her room. I smile to myself and say, "There she goes, headed into that secret place."

Mom, may I personally say that I love you with all my heart, and it was a complete honor to stretch in this way. When I think of the permanent mark you will leave on this world, it makes my heart sing and my soul smile. Let the church say amen! Amen again.

Love, Ozell's girl

ANITA JOYCE

"There is nothing more intimate than knowing your family tree."

~Louis Gates Jr. PhD

This family tree is a masterpiece

Her children arise and call her blessed, her husband also, and he praises her, "Many women do noble things, but you surpass them all." Charm is deceptive, and beauty is fleeting; but a woman who fears the Lord is to be praised.

~Psalm 31:28-30

Raw journal notes

I Truly found out that there were nothing in this world could replace the emptiness that one feel when he is not a Christian. After I accepted Christ I have never felt so fulfilled after I was accepted Christ in my life. It was at first I did not know what it meant to recieve Christ. I was raised in the COGIC where people were knocked out under the power of God, so I did not know that I saw the power that caused the slaying in the spirit. So I fell out and but I did not recieve the power of God in my life that night. So I was not sure of my salvation. I left and did not come back for a while because I relly had doubts in my heart about my ~~actual~~ salvation. But my sister alee came over to see me and she ask me some very important

questions about my salvation,
Concerning my mind at the time
She asked did I yet have the same
desires or sinful desires I had?
I said no because I was a some
women who spoke her mind and
was not afraid of any one. So
I have different feeling about how
I talked not using my bad language
and ready to fight anyone at
any time. When we got through
talking I decided to return to
Church and when I did God be
gan to bless me to grow because
I w serious about wanting to
Know God. meanwhile, Elder
Uta Smith came to our church
for a revival and at that time
The Holy Gost used him mightelty
He began to preach and sing
The Spirit of God came upon
me and filled me with the
Holy Gost and I have not
had any doubt in my heart since

I speak of a women who has given her self all of her life since she was a small child, first she took Care of her folks when she was 9-10 years old. Her father had ulsers so bad until he almost died. But God spaired his life. He was in the Shreepot Charity Haspital for many week while they were trying to find a Cure for usler. Finally they sent him home, he wo had lost so much weight be couse he could not keep any food on his stomach. We lived with my sister ale and celles Steel because we were trying to relocate from the County of Shanyoo to Haynsville La. My dad almost died in the Haspital, but when he came home there were no one to take care of him but me I would stay by his side day and night, giving him something to try get to stay on his stomach. Soup, broth warm milk. I remembered giving in flour and water to keep him from food going through him. My dad give up and went back to the Country, but he left me to stay with my sister, later we got a letter for my dad that they had found The hospital wanted him to come back and allow them treat him, but he had

210

"God Of The Second Chance"

Why is this called the Farrell and Billy R. Salar Ship Fund?

Because these two young men had a passion for young people, who had strayed away from their training.

They both were borned in the Church, their father a Pastor. They were trained and went to school. They were trained in Cub Scott, Little Ligue and *Boy's Club,* Jr. Oleph. Both boys were high achievers in schooll who got many awards and certificates.

They were also trained well in the Church. They both sanged in the Sunshine Band choir, *B.Y.P.U.* Jr. Choir, because God gifted Billy with a big *youth* gift to sang. They both had many friends *choir* who had great influence on them, some of them did not attend Church. So they went out to find the missing parts, that they through they were miissing ✱

So they became the <u>Prodical</u> Sons in <u>Luke</u> 15:11-32 This son asked for his portion, and his father gave it to him, and he went out and wasted his "inheritage". But one good part he came to himself. So did these two young men. They came to themselfes. So they came home to work with <u>passion</u>, and <u>Commitment</u> to work *(looking* for God. He came back with the song in his heart *for a* Billy formed an Organization called The *miracle* <u>Wings of Freedom</u>. This Organization was *over)* comitted to helping young people stay out of trouble, giving them employment But there were much dedication on their part. Thursday night Bible Class, Sunday morning Sunday School *Service* the bus was loaded Coming to Church, some time the second load, spreading the gospel of Jesus

The God Of A Second Chance

Billy was a great witness for God in the streets and in door to door Christ. While Lorell worked by "Wrap Sessions" And Telephone witnessing. Lorell worked as a deacon in the Church And Billy was able to became a Ordian Elder in the Church. All becouse he work for God with passion. As I look out into the auditorm tonight I can see some one who this young man changed And they are yet Serving in the Church.

Why am I telling you this Story? to let you know God is a God of the "Second Chance." And that you have a great oppetunity to go to school, and stay in School, and give your self the Gift of Education.

Go to college, find the missing part of your life. Tell your self I will succeed, in my life.

If you are a drop out, go back to school and make good your second chance

Photo Gallery

Me celebrating Black Heritage Day

A.D. and I after a Sunday service

Wow! Vacation Time

Ozell waiting for the kids to finish playing at the St. Rita's Bazaar

Ozell enjoying a day at the beach with her girls. Courtesy of Steve Cooper, Jr Photography

BIBLIOGRAPHY

ABS Staff. 2015. "10 Outrageous Reasons Black People Were Lynched in America." *Atlanta Black Star*, February 14, 2014. http://atlantablack-star.com/2014/02/14/10-outrageous-reasons-black-people-were-lynched-in-america/2/.

Bible Gateway. 2017. All Scriptures throughout Josie's Girl. https://www.biblegateway.com/.

"Calisphere: 1921–Present: Modern California—Migration, Technology." 2005. https://calisphere.org/exhibitions/essay/7/modern-california/.

"Church of God in Christ, Memphis (1907–)." *The Black Past*. www.black-past.org.

Encyclopedia of Arkansas, s.v. "Malaria." 2011. www.encyclopediaofar-kansas.net/encyclopedia/entry-detail.aspx?entryID=4780.

"Eucalyptus." University of Maryland. 1997. http://www.umm.edu/health/medical/altmed/herb/eucalyptus

"FDR Creates the WPA." History.com, 2009. http://www.history.com/this-day-in-history/fdr-creates-the-wpa#.

Hammond, Fred. *Mills of Co Offaly: An Industrial Heritage Survey*. Offaly County Council, Offaly, Ireland 2009. www.offaly.ie/eng/Services/Heritage/Documents/offaly_mills_1.pdf.

Holiday, Billie. "Strange Fruit." www.azlyrics.com.

"Jim Crow Laws—United States American History." www.u-s-history.com/pages/h1559.html.

"Juneteenth." Texas State Library and Archives Commission. https://www.tsl.texas.gov/ref/abouttx/juneteenth.htm.

Lincoln, Abraham. "The Gettysburg Address." Abraham Lincoln Online, November 19, 1863. www.abrahamlincolnonline.org/lincoln/speeches/gettysburg.htm.

"Maternal and Child Health." ONE, 2015. https://www.one.org/international/issues/maternal-and-child-health/.

"Native American Heritage Month—Recipes." First Nations. www.firstnations.org/recipes.

Nickerson, A., R. A. Bryant, I. M. Aderka, D. E. Hinton, and S. G. Hofmann. "The Impacts of Parental Loss and Adverse Parenting on Mental Health: Findings from the National Comorbidity Survey-Replication." *Psychological Trauma: Theory, Research, Practice, and Policy*. Advance online publication (2011, October 17). Digital Object Identifier. https://doi.org/10.1037/a0025695.

"Old Shongaloo Populated Place Profile/Webster Parish, Louisiana Data." 2017. www.louisiana.hometownlocator.com.

"Peace Bonds." Law Facts. www.lawfacts.ca/criminal/peace-bonds.

"Preeclampsia and Eclampsia: Risk Factors, Signs & Symptoms." WebMD, 2016. www.webmd.com/baby/guide/preeclampsia-eclampsia.

Van Rijn, Guido. *Roosevelt's Blues: African-American Blues and Gospel Songs on FDR*. University of Mississippi Press, 1995. Oxford, Mississippi

"Sharecropping: The Failure of Reconstruction." History.com. www.history.com/topics/black-history/sharecropping.

Teranisi, Robert. *Black Residential Migration in California: Implications for Higher Education Policy*. Research & Policy Institute of California, 2015. www.steinhardt.nyu.edu/scmsAdmin/uploads/005/841/RTT_RPIC.pdf.

"Thirteenth Amendment—Black History." History.com. www.history.com/topics/black-history/thirteenth-amendment.

"Washington, Glover." Celebrating Family Unity (The descendants of Addie Washington-Doss and Josie Glover-Greer, 2010).

"W. E. B. DuBois—Does the Negro Need Separate Schools?" National Humanities Center, 2007. http://nationalhumanitiescenter.org/tserve/freedom/1917beyond/essays/does-the-negro-need-seperate-schools.pdf

"Western Migration—AAME—In Motion: The African-American Migration Experience." 2005. http://www.inmotionaame.org/print.cfm?migration=6

ABOUT THE AUTHOR

Dr. Ozell Greer-Cooper is a passionate and driven woman of God. Christ centered, a child advocate, and a lover of life, she is a nurturing mother, grandmother, great-grandmother, and great-great-grandmother. She lives by the mantra that "I can do all things through Christ who strengthens me."

She is a lifelong teacher and a lover of knowledge. She first received Christ at the Looney Street COGIC in Shreveport, Louisiana, under the leadership of B. T. Kirkpatrick. Her first calling came after she was filled with the Holy Spirit. She was appointed as a Bible Band teacher and later became a Sunday-School teacher and served in that post until she moved to West Texas. There she sang in the choir and served on the usher board.

In 1955 she and her family moved to San Diego, California, where she became active at the House of Refuge COGIC under the leadership of Elder A. D. Kirkpatrick. There she served as general secretary, sanctuary choir president, and pastor's aide. In the Calvary District, she served as usher board president and Bible Band president.

In 1963 her husband, then-elder A. D. Cooper, founded the Greater Antioch COGIC. She served as president of the women's department and adviser to women and youth. She is an advocate for children and literacy and volunteered at literacy programs in her Southeast San Diego neighborhood, where she lived for over sixty years. She founded the Christian Community Intercessory Prayer Team and is currently serving as State Chaplain and member of the State Women's Department Examining Board for the Second Ecclesiastical Jurisdiction.

Dr. Ozell received her Associate's Degree in Child Development from San Diego City College, a Bachelor's Degree in Bible studies from Trinity Theological Seminary, and an Honorary Doctoral Degree from American Urban University. She has also received numerous certificates and commendations for her many years of service in the San Diego area. In May of 2003, she was honored as Mother of the Year by Delta Sigma Theta.

Dr. Cooper was married to her husband, the late Superintendent A. D. Cooper, for seventy-two years and ten months. Together they have nine children, twenty-two grandchildren, thirty-eight great-grandchildren, and ten great-great-grandchildren. She currently lives in San Diego, California.

Made in the USA
San Bernardino,
CA